LENT 2019

DEVOTIONAL

CITY PRESBYTERIAN CHURCH

Published by White Blackbird Books, an imprint of Storied Publishing

Permission requests and other questions may be directed to the Contact page at www.storied.pub.

The entries were written by members of City Presbyterian Church in Oklahoma City. Edited by Catie Forester.

Wes Martin | Kaitlin Martin | April Spencer | Jake Spencer | Sara Hawk | Allison Brown | Becky Carlozzi | Josh Spears | Catie Forester | Bobby Griffith | Hannah Barrett | Alison Buxton | Erika Forrest | Doug Serven | Matt Teeselink | Melissa Whittaker | Keely Steger

CONTENTS

ABOUT THIS LENTEN DEVOTIONAL

Since the early days of the church Lent has been a season of self-examination, sorrow for sin, and a commitment—a season for renewal. Lent lasts for forty days plus six Sundays. Sundays are not included because the Lord's Day, according to church tradition, is never a fast day but always a feast day, a celebration of the resurrection.

The word "lent" comes from an old German word that meant "long" and is connected to a long Spring.

Lent is traditionally observed by penitence, almsgiving, self-denial, and, above all, prayer. We humble ourselves before God, coming before him in dust and ashes, confessing our sin and total inadequacy, stripping ourselves bare of all pretense to righteousness. We place our needs, fear, failures, hopes and lives into the hands of God. We confess that our only hope is in Christ, who lived, died, and rose on our behalf.

During this season, Christians are urged to pray and meditate on the Gospel accounts of the passion, death, and resurrection of Jesus Christ. Lent may or may not be familiar to you. It has been a time in the church calendar when Christians prepared for Easter Sunday, our greatest celebration of the resurrection of our Lord and Savior Jesus Christ. However, in the rush to get to Easter, we often forget the life and ministry of Jesus. We often forget he was the Suffering Servant. We love his grace and goodness, but we forget his pain and heartbreak. Lent helps remind us; it helps prepare us.

Some have given something up—not something trivial, but something you hold dear. This doesn't make you more worthy of grace, but reminds you that you can direct your desires and wants toward something different. Don't make this a badge of honor or hold your denial as some sort of goodness. Please consider also what you might start doing during this time: reading the gospels, memorizing Scripture, or giving to the poor could be new things to begin during Lent. Some have started attending a City-Group or started going on prayer walks during lunch. Some have fasted one day or one meal of the week. Join us as we prepare for Easter Sunday, not as we make ourselves better or more worthy. It's as we better see our unworthiness and his beauty in his pain on our behalf.

As Jesus made clear when he quoted Isaiah to the Pharisees, external actions void of heart engagement are not honoring to God: *"This people honors me with their lips, but their heart is far from me."* (Matthew 15:8) Therefore, any special attention to the Lenten Season that honors God must include heart-level repentance and real faith, not external obedience to church tradition.

In this book you will find a reading for each day from Ash Wednesday until Easter. Our hope is that as you read the Scriptures and meditate on their meaning you will identify more fully with Christ in what he did on the cross, and what he continues to do for us today.

WEEK 1

WEEPING & CLEANSING (LUKE 19)

LUKE 19

Jesus and Zacchaeus

19 HE ENTERED JERICHO AND WAS PASSING THROUGH. 2 And behold, there was a man named Zacchaeus. He was a chief tax collector and was rich. 3 And he was seeking to see who Jesus was, but on account of the crowd he could not, because he was small in stature. 4 So he ran on ahead and climbed up into a sycamore tree to see him, for he was about to pass that way. 5 And when Jesus came to the place, he looked up and said to him, "Zacchaeus, hurry and come down, for I must stay at your house today." 6 So he hurried and came down and received him joyfully. 7 And when they saw it, they all grumbled, "He has gone in to be the guest of a man who is a sinner." 8 And Zacchaeus stood and said to the Lord, "Behold, Lord, the half of my goods I give to the poor. And if I have defrauded anyone of anything, I restore it fourfold." 9 And Jesus said to him, "Today salvation has come to this

house, since he also is a son of Abraham. 10 For the Son of Man came to seek and to save the lost."

The Parable of the Ten Minas

11 As they heard these things, he proceeded to tell a parable, because he was near to Jerusalem, and because they supposed that the kingdom of God was to appear immediately. 12 He said therefore, "A nobleman went into a far country to receive for himself a kingdom and then return. 13 Calling ten of his servants, he gave them ten minas, and said to them, 'Engage in business until I come.' 14 But his citizens hated him and sent a delegation after him, saying, 'We do not want this man to reign over us.' 15 When he returned, having received the kingdom, he ordered these servants to whom he had given the money to be called to him, that he might know what they had gained by doing business. 16 The first came before him, saying, 'Lord, your mina has made ten minas more.' 17 And he said to him, 'Well done, good servant! Because you have been faithful in a very little, you shall have authority over ten cities.' 18 And the second came, saying, 'Lord, your mina has made five minas.' 19 And he said to him, 'And you are to be over five cities.' 20 Then another came, saying, 'Lord, here is your mina, which I kept laid away in a handkerchief; 21 for I was afraid of you, because you are a severe man. You take what you did not deposit, and reap what you did not sow.' 22 He said to him, 'I will condemn you with your own words, you wicked servant! You knew that I was a severe man, taking what I did not deposit and reaping what I did not sow?

23 Why then did you not put my money in the bank, and at my coming I might have collected it with interest?' 24 And he said to those who stood by, 'Take the mina from him, and give it to the one who has the ten minas.' 25 And they said to him, 'Lord, he has ten minas!' 26 'I tell you that to everyone who has, more will be given, but from the one who has not, even what he has will be taken away. 27 But as for these enemies of mine, who did not want me to reign over them, bring them here and slaughter them before me.'"

The Triumphal Entry

28 And when he had said these things, he went on ahead, going up to Jerusalem. 29 When he drew near to Bethphage and Bethany, at the mount that is called Olivet, he sent two of the disciples, 30 saying, "Go into the village in front of you, where on entering you will find a colt tied, on which no one has ever yet sat. Untie it and bring it here. 31 If anyone asks you, 'Why are you untying it?' you shall say this: 'The Lord has need of it.'" 32 So those who were sent went away and found it just as he had told them. 33 And as they were untying the colt, its owners said to them, "Why are you untying the colt?" 34 And they said, "The Lord has need of it." 35 And they brought it to Jesus, and throwing their cloaks on the colt, they set Jesus on it. 36 And as he rode along, they spread their cloaks on the road. 37 As he was drawing near—already on the way down the Mount of Olives—the whole multitude of his disciples began to rejoice and praise God with a loud voice for all the mighty works that they had seen,

38 saying, "Blessed is the King who comes in the name of the Lord! Peace in heaven and glory in the highest!" 39 And some of the Pharisees in the crowd said to him, "Teacher, rebuke your disciples." 40 He answered, "I tell you, if these were silent, the very stones would cry out."

Jesus Weeps over Jerusalem

41 And when he drew near and saw the city, he wept over it, 42 saying, "Would that you, even you, had known on this day the things that make for peace! But now they are hidden from your eyes. 43 For the days will come upon you, when your enemies will set up a barricade around you and surround you and hem you in on every side 44 and tear you down to the ground, you and your children within you. And they will not leave one stone upon another in you, because you did not know the time of your visitation."

Jesus Cleanses the Temple

45 And he entered the temple and began to drive out those who sold, 46 saying to them, "It is written, 'My house shall be a house of prayer,' but you have made it a den of robbers."

47 And he was teaching daily in the temple. The chief priests and the scribes and the principal men of the people were seeking to destroy him, 48 but they did not find anything they could do, for all the people were hanging on his words.

ASH WEDNESDAY

A CHURCH SERVICE

ASH WEDNESDAY IS A DAY OF SOLEMN ASSEMBLY that is built into the church year. It is a fast day, a day of mourning for our sin and the sin of all humanity before God, a recognition of our mortality save for the grace of God and a request that the Lord remember our creation and breathe new life into our burned-out, dusty lives once more.

Opening Prayer

Let us pray.
Almighty and everlasting God, you hate nothing you have made and forgive the sins of all who are penitent: Create and make in us new and contrite hearts, that we, worthily lamenting our sins and acknowledging our wickedness, may obtain of you, the God of all mercy, perfect remission and forgiveness; through Jesus Christ our Lord, who lives

and reigns with you and the Holy Spirit, one God, for ever and ever.

Our Father, who is in heaven, hallowed be your name. Your kingdom come; your will be done on earth as it is in heaven. Give us this day our daily bread, and forgive us our debts as we forgive our debtors. Lead us not into temptation, but deliver us from evil. For yours is the kingdom and the power and the glory forever and ever. Amen.

Old Testament Reading

1 Blow a trumpet in Zion; sound an alarm on my holy mountain! Let all the inhabitants of the land tremble, for the day of the Lord is coming; it is near, 2 a day of darkness and gloom, a day of clouds and thick darkness! Like blackness there is spread upon the mountains a great and powerful people; their like has never been before, nor will be again after them through the years of all generations. 12 "Yet even now," declares the Lord, "return to me with all your heart, with fasting, with weeping, and with mourning; 13 and rend your hearts and not your garments.â€ Return to the Lord your God, for he is gracious and merciful, slow to anger, and abounding in steadfast love; and he relents over disaster. 14 Who knows whether he will not turn and relent, and leave a blessing

behind him, a grain offering and a drink offering for the Lord your God? 15 Blow the trumpet in Zion; consecrate a fast; call a solemn assembly; 16 gather the people. Consecrate the congregation; assemble the elders; gather the children, even nursing infants. Let the bridegroom leave his room, and the bride her chamber. 17 Between the vestibule and the altar let the priests, the ministers of the Lord, weep and say, "Spare your people, O Lord, and make not your heritage a reproach, a byword among the nations. Why should they say among the peoples, "Where is their God?" *Joel* 2:*1-2, 12-17*

Abide With Me, Henry Lyte, 1843

Abide with me; falls the eventide;
the darkness deepens; Lord with me abide.
When other helpers, fail and comforts flee,
help of the helpless, abide with me.

Thou on my head, in early youth didst smile;
and, though rebellious, and perverse meanwhile,
Thou hast not left me, oft as I left Thee,
on to the close Lord, abide with me.

I need Thy presence, every passing hour.
What but Thy grace, can foil the tempter's power?
Who, like Thyself, my guide and stay can be?
Through cloud and sunshine, abide with me.

I fear no foe, with Thee at hand to bless,
ills have no weight, tears lose their bitterness
Where is thy sting death? Where grave thy victory?
I triumph still, abide with me.

Hold Thou Thy cross, before my closing eyes;
shine through the gloom, and point me to the skies.
Heaven's morning breaks, and earth's vain shadows flee;
in life, in death, Lord, abide with me.

New Testament Reading

Therefore, we are ambassadors for Christ, God making his appeal through us. We implore you on behalf of Christ, be reconciled to God. 2 1 For our sake he made him to be sin who knew no sin, so that in him we might become the righteousness of God. 6 Working together with him, then, we appeal to you not to receive the grace of God in vain. 2 For he says, "In a favorable time I listened to you, and in a day of salvation I have helped you." Behold, now is the favorable time; behold, now is the day of salvation. 3 We put no obstacle in anyone's way, so that no fault may be found with our ministry, 4 but as servants of God we commend ourselves in every way: by great endurance, in afflictions, hardships, calamities, 5 beatings, imprisonments, riots, labors, sleepless nights, hunger; 6 by purity, knowledge, patience, kindness, the Holy Spirit, genuine love; 7 by truthful speech, and the power of God; with the weapons of righteousness for the right hand and for the left; 8 through honor and dishonor, through slander and praise. We are treated as impostors, and yet are true; 9 as unknown, and yet well known; as dying, and behold, we live; as punished, and yet not killed; 10 as sorrowful, yet always rejoicing; as poor, yet making many rich; as having nothing, yet possessing everything. *1 Corinthians 5:20-6:10*

Gospel Reading

6 Beware of practicing your righteousness before other people in order to be seen by them, for then you will have no reward from your Father who is in heaven. 2 Thus, when you give to the needy, sound no trumpet before you, as the hypocrites do in the synagogues and in the streets, that they may be praised by others. Truly, I say to you, they have received their reward. 3 But when you give to the needy, do not let your left hand know what your right hand is doing, 4 so that your giving may be in secret. And your Father who sees in secret will reward you. 5 â€œAnd when you pray, you must not be like the hypocrites. For they love to stand and pray in the synagogues and at the street corners, that they may be seen by others. Truly, I say to you, they have received their reward. 6 But when you pray, go into your room and shut the door and pray to your Father who is in secret. And your Father who sees in secret will reward you. 16 And when you fast, do not look gloomy like the hypocrites, for they disfigure their faces that their fasting may be seen by others. Truly, I say to you, they have received their reward. 17 But when you fast, anoint your head and wash your face, 18 that your

fasting may not be seen by others but by your Father who is in secret. And your Father who sees in secret will reward you. 19 Do not lay up for yourselves treasures on earth, where moth and rust destroy and where thieves break in and steal, 20 but lay up for yourselves treasures in heaven, where neither moth nor rust destroys and where thieves do not break in and steal. 21 For where your treasure is, there your heart will be also. *Matthew 6:1-6, 16-21*

Homily

Imposition of Ashes

Dear People of God: The first Christians observed with great devotion the days of our Lord's passion and resurrection, and it became the custom of the Church to prepare for them by a season of penitence and fasting. This season of Lent provided a time in which converts to the faith were prepared for Holy Baptism. It was also a time when those who, because of notorious sins, had been separated from the body of the faithful were reconciled by penitence and forgiveness, and restored to the fellowship of the Church. Thereby, the whole congregation was put in mind of the message of pardon and absolution set forth in the Gospel of our Savior, and of the need which all Christians continually have to renew their repentance and faith. I invite you, therefore to the observance of a holy Lent, by self-examination and repentance; by prayer, fasting, and self-denial; and by reading and meditating on God's holy Word. And, to make a right beginning of repentance, and as a mark of our mortal nature, let us now kneel before the Lord, our maker and redeemer.

Almighty God, you have created us out of the dust of the earth: Grant that these ashes may be to us a sign of our mortality and penitence, that we may remember that it is only by your gracious gift that we are given everlasting life; through Jesus Christ our Savior.

Amen.

God Be Merciful to Me (Psalm 51)

God, be merciful to me;
On Thy grace I rest my plea
Plenteous in compassion Thou,
Blot out my transgressions now;
Wash me, make me pure within;
Cleanse, O cleanse me from my sin.

My transgressions I confess;
Grief and guilt my soul oppress.
I have sinned against Thy grace,
And provoked Thee to Thy face.
I confess Thy judgement just;
Speechless, I Thy mercy trust.

I am evil, born in sin;
Thou desirest truth within.
Thou alone my Savior art,

Teach Thy wisdom to my heart;
Make me pure, Thy grace bestow,
Wash me whiter than the snow.

Broken, humbled to the dust
By Thy wrath and judgment just,
Let my contrite heart rejoice,
And in gladness hear Thy voice;
From my sins O hide Thy face,
Blot them out in boundless grace.

Gracious God, my heart renew,
Make my spirit right and true.
Cast me not away from Thee,
Let Thy Spirit dwell in me;
Thy salvation's joy impart,
Steadfast make my willing heart.

Sinners then shall learn from me,
And return, O God, to Thee
Savior all my guilt remove,
And my tongue shall sing Thy love
Touch my silent lips, O Lord,
And my mouth shall praise accord

Litany of Penitence

Most holy and merciful Father: We confess to you
and to one another that we have sinned by our own
fault in thought, word, and deed; by what we have

done, and by what we have left undone. We have not loved you with our whole heart, and mind, and strength. We have not loved our neighbors as ourselves. We have not forgiven others, as we have been forgiven.

Have mercy on us, Lord.

We have been deaf to your call to serve, as Christ served us. We have not been true to the mind of Christ. We have grieved your Holy Spirit.

Have mercy on us, Lord.

We confess to you, Lord, all our past unfaithfulness: the pride, hypocrisy, and impatience of our lives,

We confess to you, Lord.

Our self-indulgent appetites and ways, and our exploitation of other people,

We confess to you, Lord.

Our anger at our own frustration, and our envy of those more fortunate than ourselves,

We confess to you, Lord.

Our intemperate love of worldly goods and comforts, and our dishonesty in daily life and work,

We confess to you, Lord.

Our negligence in prayer and worship, and our failure to commend the faith that is in us,

We confess to you, Lord.

Accept our repentance, Lord, for the wrongs we have done: for our blindness to human need and suffering, and our indifference to injustice and cruelty,

Accept our repentance, Lord.

For all false judgments, for uncharitable thoughts toward

our neighbors, and for our prejudice and contempt toward those who differ from us,

Accept our repentance, Lord.

For our waste and pollution of your creation, and our lack of concern for those who come after us,

Accept our repentance, Lord.

Restore us, good Lord, and let your anger depart from us;

Favorably hear us, for your mercy is great.

Accomplish in us the work of your salvation,

That we may show forth your glory in the world.

By the cross and passion of your Son our Lord,

Bring us with all your saints to the joy of his resurrection.

Almighty God, the Father of our Lord Jesus Christ, who desires not the death of sinners, but rather that they may turn from their wickedness and live, has given power and commandment to his ministers to declare and pronounce to his people, being penitent, the absolution and remission of their sins. He pardons and absolves all those who truly repent, and with sincere hearts believe his holy Gospel. Therefore we beseech him to grant us true repentance and his Holy Spirit, that those things may please him which we do on this day, and that the rest of our life here-after may be pure and holy, so that at the last we may come to his eternal joy; through Jesus Christ our Lord. Amen.

Benediction

Let us go forth and serve Oklahoma City and the world through Jesus Christ our Lord; who was in every way tempted as we are, yet did not sin; by whose grace we are able to triumph over every evil, and to live no longer unto ourselves, but unto him who died for us and rose again. Amen.

WEDNESDAY

WES MARTIN

THE IMAGE OF JESUS WEEPING OVER JERUSALEM AS he prophecies its downfall is an appropriate one for the beginning of Lent—a solemn time for us to think about our sin, where we need to repent, and where we desperately need forgiveness. Lent is the time to realize the judgment we deserve, the judgment *I* deserve for all the ways I constantly fail to love God and love others. We really don't like to think about God's judgment. I like to think of myself as a "grace" guy. And I am completely convinced that only the *love* of God (not the judgment of God) can change our hearts, save us, and make us holy. But my time working with alcoholics, addicts, and criminals has definitely taught me that there is a real and necessary place for recognizing the coming of God's judgment for those who will not repent.

Real and necessary as it may be, Jesus did not prophesy over the coming judgment in joy; he wept over it. And in the end he cared so much that he took the judgment on himself at the cross. It is as we come to realize the depths of judgment we deserve that we are all the more amazed by the even deeper love of Christ and what he did for us on the cross, which leads us to call out to Jesus for forgiveness, mercy, and salvation.

O God, have mercy on me, a sinner. I have not loved you with my whole heart, mind, soul, and strength, and I have not loved my neighbor as myself. For the sake of Jesus Christ, the one who wept for my sin and was punished for my sin, have mercy on me, convict me of sin, bring me to true repentance, true change, and restore me to the joy of knowing salvation. Bring me to weep over my sin that I may dance in the joy of your mercy and love. Amen.

THURSDAY

KAITLIN MARTIN

IN A BRIEF PASSAGE FROM LUKE 19, JESUS WEEPS over "the city," Jerusalem. Why is he weeping? Because the city's inhabitants don't know the things "that make for peace!" Jesus goes on to prophesy about the future destruction of Jerusalem when "not one stone [will be] left upon the other."

Like the city over which Jesus laments, often I am not at peace. I want what's due to me. I want respect and recognition, whether I've earned it or not. I am quick to be angry at the injustices done to me or that I see done to others. In my worst moments, I see peace as weakness because it's not fighting back with words or weapons or making my opponent smaller than me.

But Jesus weeps and comes to redeem us from anger, to teach us peace and how to weep over where we are and where we've been. He gives us hope, even in the dark places, that he will rebuild and restore what was taken and broken. And he offers us this peace that is not weakness but that can heal and honor, that brings dignity and freedom. Jesus offers it all through his suffering and death on the cross. And through his resurrection, we know that no matter who burns the city to the ground and captures God's people, whether because of literal oppression or their own sins and desires, they don't get the last say. Because the King is coming out of love for them.

Prince of Peace, make us a people who weep over how we don't know the things that make for peace, for our city that lacks peace, for our country, for the world that so desperately needs redemption and to learn your peace. We fail so often to recognize that peace is even an option, or we reject the hope that peace is possible. You've told us that you've come to make the world new again, to redeem our violence and the curse of sin and death that surrounds us all. Forgive us for being a people without peace. Please give us the grace to seek peace in ourselves and for others. Amen.

FRIDAY

APRIL SPENCER

I've been convicted about something. Actually, it's kind of slapped me in the face lately, as it turns out acknowledging something without doing anything about it isn't really a good strategy for improvement. Last year, a friend and her family went through something unimaginable. They're still going through it. Their son, beautiful and active, was suddenly injured, and their life has not been the same since. The story isn't mine to tell, but I've witnessed the way a faith that has been lived out in time spent in the word, in prayer, in loving hospitality, and community with friends, has sustained my friend. I don't think I can say the same for the way I spend a lot of my time. If faced with a similar situation, will my knowledge of the Real Housewives increase my faith? Will my time wasted on Instagram—even scrolling the accounts about books or cooking—serve to remind me of how Jesus has not left me? No, not even a little.

When Jesus came back to Jerusalem, a city he loved, before he was crucified, he wept as the people cheered for him, knowing the rejection and later destruction that were coming. I think I'm Jerusalem in this story. I'm welcoming him in on Sunday morning, or in a short quiet time or bible study, but rejecting him when convicted to go deeper. It's easy to say I'm being too hard on myself, but I think there's room for improvement. I want my first reaction to stress to be prayer and scripture recall, and that only comes from a deeper relationship with Jesus.

Jesus, give me a desire in my heart and a motivation in my mind to want to know you more. Amen.

SATURDAY

SARA HAWK

In this chapter from Luke, it always seemed to me that Jesus was just walking to Jerusalem, had this random moment where he mourned its future destruction by Rome, and then moved on to the Temple where he started flipping tables. However, in the last couple of weeks, these two seemingly separate passages have made a bit more sense to me as a cohesive whole.

Weeping and cleansing. Mourning over sin followed by a rebuke. Often we tend to lean to one more than the other. I know, in my non-confrontational heart of hearts, that I prefer to mourn over sin and leave the rebuke to someone else. Others jump on the rebuke train without even a thought to what it would mean to sit with someone who is actively in sin and weep over the choices they have made.

Jesus does not choose between the two. Rather, after his triumphal entry into the city of Jerusalem, he mourns the people's inability to see him as their Messiah. They were looking for someone to come in power to overthrow Rome. Not a "Prince of Peace" who could heal their sinful hearts and set the oppressed free. So, because they could not see him, the very thing they wanted released from will destroy them. On the other end, Jesus comes to the Temple and sees the Gentile court filled with people peddling animals for sacrifice and other things (imagine the kiosks in the mall). They were creating distractions for people who were coming to worship and Jesus rightly rebukes them. In glorious Liz Lemon fashion, Jesus says, "shut it down."

Over the last couple of weeks, I have experienced this same tension: Neighbor fighting neighbor, all people I care about, but no one completely innocent; Family members struggling once again in their battle against substance abuse. Jesus's example from Luke 19 shows us how to handle such situations. Both of these instances require mourning/weeping over the sin and a rebuke that will lead to repentance and reconciliation. After cleansing the Temple, Jesus does not leave. He stays, "teaching daily in the temple." Weeping and cleansing require our presence and commitment to see people through. During Lent, we intentionally take time to look at our sin. Where do we see Jesus in our own hearts weeping with and for us over our sin, and gently rebuking us as his children to see him? To see the peace and freedom only our Messiah can give?

Lord, thank you for your example of weeping and cleans-

ing. Let this Lenten season be a time in which we both mourn our sin and allow the conviction of the Holy Spirit to lead us to repentance and reconciliation. Thank you for making that possible. Amen.

SUNDAY FEAST DAY

REFLECTIONS ON THE LAST WEEK AND THE RESURRECTION LIFE TO COME

WEEK 2

AUTHORITY & TENANTS (LUKE 20)

LUKE 20

The Authority of Jesus Challenged

20 ONE DAY, AS JESUS WAS TEACHING THE PEOPLE IN the temple and preaching the gospel, the chief priests and the scribes with the elders came up 2 and said to him, "Tell us by what authority you do these things, or who it is that gave you this authority." 3 He answered them, "I also will ask you a question. Now tell me, 4 was the baptism of John from heaven or from man?" 5 And they discussed it with one another, saying, "If we say, 'From heaven,' he will say, 'Why did you not believe him?' 6 But if we say, 'From man,' all the people will stone us to death, for they are convinced that John was a prophet." 7 So they answered that they did not know where it came from. 8 And Jesus said to them, "Neither will I tell you by what authority I do these things."

The Parable of the Wicked Tenants

9 And he began to tell the people this parable: "A man planted a vineyard and let it out to tenants and went into another country for a long while. 10 When the time came, he sent a servant to the tenants, so that they would give him some of the fruit of the vineyard. But the tenants beat him and sent him away empty-handed. 11 And he sent another servant. But they also beat and treated him shamefully, and sent him away empty-handed. 12 And he sent yet a third. This one also they wounded and cast out. 13 Then the owner of the vineyard said, 'What shall I do? I will send my beloved son; perhaps they will respect him.' 14 But when the tenants saw him, they said to themselves, 'This is the heir. Let us kill him, so that the inheritance may be ours.' 15 And they threw him out of the vineyard and killed him. What then will the owner of the vineyard do to them? 16 He will come and destroy those tenants and give the vineyard to others." When they heard this, they said, "Surely not!" 17 But he looked directly at them and said, "What then is this that is written:

"'The stone that the builders rejected
   has become the cornerstone'?

   18 Everyone who falls on that stone will be broken to pieces, and when it falls on anyone, it will crush him."

Paying Taxes to Caesar

19 The scribes and the chief priests sought to lay hands on him at that very hour, for they perceived that he had told this parable against them, but they feared the people. 20 So they watched him and sent spies, who pretended to be sincere, that they might catch him in something he said, so as to deliver him up to the authority and jurisdiction of the governor. 21 So they asked him, "Teacher, we know that you speak and teach rightly, and show no partiality, but truly teach the way of God. 22 Is it lawful for us to give tribute to Caesar, or not?" 23 But he perceived their craftiness, and said to them, 24 "Show me a denarius. Whose likeness and inscription does it have?" They said, "Caesar's." 25 He said to them, "Then render to Caesar the things that are Caesar's, and to God the things that are God's." 26 And they were not able in the presence of the people to catch him in what he said, but marveling at his answer they became silent.

Sadducees Ask About the Resurrection

27 There came to him some Sadducees, those who deny that there is a resurrection, 28 and they asked him a question, saying, "Teacher, Moses wrote for us that if a man's brother dies, having a wife but no children, the man must take the widow and raise up offspring for his brother. 29 Now there were seven brothers. The first took a wife, and died without children. 30 And the second 31 and the third took her, and likewise all seven left no children and died. 32 Afterward the woman also died. 33 In the resur-

rection, therefore, whose wife will the woman be? For the seven had her as wife."

34 And Jesus said to them, "The sons of this age marry and are given in marriage, 35 but those who are considered worthy to attain to that age and to the resurrection from the dead neither marry nor are given in marriage, 36 for they cannot die anymore, because they are equal to angels and are sons of God, being sons[g] of the resurrection. 37 But that the dead are raised, even Moses showed, in the passage about the bush, where he calls the Lord the God of Abraham and the God of Isaac and the God of Jacob. 38 Now he is not God of the dead, but of the living, for all live to him." 39 Then some of the scribes answered, "Teacher, you have spoken well." 40 For they no longer dared to ask him any question.

Whose Son Is the Christ?

41 But he said to them, "How can they say that the Christ is David's son? 42 For David himself says in the Book of Psalms,

"'The Lord said to my Lord,
"Sit at my right hand,
43 until I make your enemies your footstool.'"

44 David thus calls him Lord, so how is he his son?"

Beware of the Scribes

45 And in the hearing of all the people he said to his disciples, 46 "Beware of the scribes, who like to walk around in long robes, and love greetings in the marketplaces and the best seats in the synagogues and the places of honor at feasts, 47 who devour widows' houses and for a pretense make long prayers. They will receive the greater condemnation."

MONDAY

WES MARTIN

THE CHIEF PRIESTS AND SCRIBES WERE OBVIOUSLY starting to suspect Jesus was from God, but they didn't want Jesus interfering with their agenda: *What about us? We have a way of knowing what the Bible says and yet finding convenient ways to get around it and make excuses.*

Not the way Jesus got around the priests and scribes questions, but the way the priests and scribes were trying to keep Jesus at bay and not have to accept what Jesus and the Bible actually say, because it meant they might not get what they wanted.

And when we start saying that we have to obey Jesus and the Bible, that he is the ultimate and highest authority, others might not like that either. It can be a real challenge to love people while obeying Jesus, and maybe even making his authority known. There will be sacrifices and losses along the way. We'll make mistakes (I certainly have), but in the end, Jesus is the authority of all.

In what ways do we "challenge" Jesus like the priests

and scribes. If your answer to that question makes you a little nervous as you think about how you use your money, your sex life, your position in society, there's good news: While Jesus is the stone of judgment, he is also, thanks be to God, a merciful savior. He is the Son who willingly gives himself over to the false vine-dressers in order to be punished for our sins.

Jesus, I am a rebel, a rule avoider, a technicality finder, and often do not gladly receive what you have to say. Save me and change me, Lord. Holy Spirit, give me a heart that gladly accepts what the Bible teaches. O Lord, open my lips and my mouth will proclaim your praise. Teach me your ways, show me your mercy, and I will share your word with others. Help me do that. Thank you that you forgive a Pharisee like me. In Jesus's name, amen.

TUESDAY

ALLISON BROWN

AFTER JESUS ENTERS JERUSALEM AND CLEARS THE temple, the chief priests, elders, and scribes challenge his authority. Then, after this tense exchange, Jesus teaches the people through the parable of the wicked tenants. The priests, elders, and scribes scoff at Jesus's teachings. I often read these passages in Luke 20 with a smug sense of understanding and condescension. *Of course* Jesus has authority. *Of course* the tenants were wicked and should be destroyed. *Of course* the vineyard should be given to other tenants.

But my smugness dissipates when I ask: haven't I questioned Jesus's authority? How often have I been given love and grace, only to reject it over and over? How often have I missed the obvious point—missed *Jesus*?

I, like the servants in the parable, reject opportunities God gives to me—opportunities to grow, serve, love, and sacrifice. I, too, don't realize when God pursues me with his abundant love, over and over again. To combat my tendency to forget, ignore, and reject, I turn to a cherished lesson a mentor taught me about the spiritual practice of remembering. She encouraged me to look back over a season of life and reflect on how God was faithful, from great successes to periods of deep anxiety, to everyday disappointments and times of great joy. Remembering and recognizing these moments give me a glimpse of God's relentless pursuit of me and his faithfulness to his people.

Jesus, thank you for pursuing us with your love and grace. Open our eyes to your faithfulness in our lives.

WEDNESDAY

BECKY CARLOZZI

In Luke 20:9–18, Jesus tells the chief priests, scribes, and elders a parable about a vineyard owner and wicked tenants that concludes with the audience of Jesus's story wanting to immediately kill him. Jesus has a way of getting to the crux of matters quickly, and disproportionate anger from his listeners is often the response that we find in the Gospels, as well as in our lives today.

The Jewish leaders are enraged upon hearing that the owner of the vineyard returns to destroy the evil tenants and give the vineyard to others. After all, the tenants did beat three of the master's servants and kill the owner's son when he had sent them to get some fruit from his own vineyard. From an objective perspective, the owner's response seems justified and reasonable. But the listeners had perceived that Jesus had told the parable against them (Luke 20:19). As often happens to me when my reputation and what I think I deserve are challenged, the listeners' shame snowballs rapidly into contempt and anger.

I am beginning to learn that anger can be a guide. Following the thread of my anger backwards can connect me to the load-bearing walls of my self-constructed identity. It can illuminate where I, just like the original hearers of this parable, have rejected Christ as my cornerstone and built my own cornerstones instead. Here, I can attest that the weight of God's judgment is crushing, but praise be to God for the hope we have in Christ:

> *"therefore thus says the Lord God, 'Behold, I am the one who has laid as a foundation in Zion, a stone, a tested stone, a precious cornerstone, of a sure foundation: 'Whoever believes will not be in haste'"* Isaiah 28:16

Lord, you are a God that doesn't waste anything. You use our failures to lead us back to you. Slow us down so that we can see what you are teaching us. When we are tempted to despair because of our angry outbursts originating from our fragile identities, lead us back to faith in you as our tested and precious cornerstone.

THURSDAY

JOSH SPEARS

THEY'D BEEN AT IT FOR YEARS. YOU'D THINK THEY'D
have learned by now. The Pharisees. The Sadducees. The
Scribes. Their quest to entrap Jesus into saying and doing
things for which they could charge him with a capital
crime. To rid themselves of this thorn in their side. They
tried all manner of maneuvers. They tried to test their
mental mettle against his. They tried biblical theology.
They tried political theology. They tried passive aggres-
sive rationalist manipulation. All to no avail. The only
result a growing frustration boiling into bitterness trans-
forming into wrath and plotting to kill him. *What gives
him the right! By whose authority do you do these things?!
Who died and made you king!*

How often do I struggle with this Authoritative
Christ? The One who makes absolute claims on me? Who
upturns my tables? Who won't answer my direct questions directly? Who won't be the Christ *I* want him to be?
Isn't this, in the end, what's at stake?

Jesus just doesn't turn out to be who I want—the kind

of savior I think I need. And how often I seek to trick him into slipping up so I can reclaim that lost authority, that crushed autonomy, that sense of the world turning upside down. How quickly I do it by turning to my own understanding and wisdom and knowledge—my perception of the world. It seems much easier to remain in charge by having all the answers.

It's funny that cognitive rest comes only after I've said, *Thy will be done. Thy kingdom come.* Only in laying down my life and my questions and my rational manipulations will I find that true rest in the true Wisdom of Christ.

O Spirit of Wisdom, Who enlivened the mind of Christ to wisdom, grant the same in us your servants that we may humbly submit and faithfully follow the Christ in both his death and his resurrection, by Whom and with Whom, You and the Father, reign over all things, ever one God, world without end. Amen.

FRIDAY

CATIE FORESTER

In some ways, we are a culture obsessed with proving qualifications. In other ways, we are a culture obsessed with rejecting expertise. Just like the chief priests and the scribes who question Jesus in Luke 20, we want it both ways. *Prove yourself,* in one breath—*What do you know?* in the next.

When I'm the one in a position of authority, my tendency is to go toward the first extreme, doing everything I can to prove my bona fides and show how well equipped I am to be in charge. When I am the one coming under authority, I tend toward the other extreme. It may not appear that way on the outside, but in my heart and in my mind I want to reject the claims of authority over me and the responsibility that comes with those claims.

Why am I like this? Why do I fear being held accountable? Because I know I don't measure up. I fail the people I'm in charge of and I fail the people in charge of me. Like the chief priests and scribes, I falsely believe I can effort myself to a position of legitimate authority when I'm the one in charge—if I can just read enough books or find the best strategies, I'll solve all my children's problems and be the perfect mom. Also like the ones who question Jesus in this passage, I am made uncomfortable by the notion of having to answer to anyone but myself, which manifests itself in a tendency to be skeptical or even critical of those who have been placed in authority over me.

But I can learn from Jesus's response in this passage. He doesn't fall for the trap that has been set for him, and I don't have to, either. I do have to admit that relying on my own efforts to lead and follow well will always come up short and put my faith in Jesus, the one whose life demonstrated what it means to lead and be led, perfectly.

Lord, thank you for your sinless life of servant leadership and willing submission. I'm sorry for the ways I have neither led nor followed well. By your grace and the power of the Holy Spirit, help me to grow toward your example as I continue walk out my various callings to lead and follow. Amen.

SATURDAY

BOBBY GRIFFITH

I REMEMBER GETTING INTO A SCUFFLE WITH MY DAD near the end of my high school days; I started it. We were putting up a fence around a field and he asked me to do something. I balked at being ordered around and puffed my chest. For a brief moment, it seemed like we would fight. We did not, of course. As I reflect upon that event, I realize that I knew his authority over my life was passing. I was "coming of age," and on the cusp of college and adulthood. I was ready to be the one in charge of my life, rather than my father. We often balk at authority because it is temporary. Parents, presidents, governors, and bosses, are all "term limited." Doctor's orders are for a short time. Nations and kingdoms fall to the wayside. We also tend to view authority with a negative connotation, merely as something with the power to impose consequences.

When Jesus came to usher in the Kingdom of God, it astonished people. The religious experts could not believe he taught with such command. Look at the people he healed! Look at the people to whom he gave up his time!

Surely he cannot possess the authority with which he teaches! But that was precisely the point. The coming of God's Kingdom was a reimagining of authority. A kingdom of love and mercy and justice built upon a foundation of righteousness that flowed from the King himself. Jesus, the rejected cornerstone is the foundation of life and possesses an authority we cannot fully comprehend because it flies against our very nature.

Jesus Christ, Lord and Giver of life. Help me to follow your way and rest in the authority that has been committed to you. Amen.

SUNDAY FEAST DAY

REFLECTIONS ON THE LAST WEEK AND THE RESURRECTION LIFE TO COME

WEEK THREE

LUKE 21

The Widow's Offering

21 JESUS LOOKED UP AND SAW THE RICH PUTTING their gifts into the offering box, 2 and he saw a poor widow put in two small copper coins. 3 And he said, "Truly, I tell you, this poor widow has put in more than all of them. 4 For they all contributed out of their abundance, but she out of her poverty put in all she had to live on."

Jesus Foretells Destruction of the Temple

5 And while some were speaking of the temple, how it was adorned with noble stones and offerings, he said, 6 "As for these things that you see, the days will come when there will not be left here one stone upon another that will not be thrown down." 7 And they asked him, "Teacher, when will these things be, and what will be the sign when these things are about to take place?" 8 And he

said, "See that you are not led astray. For many will come in my name, saying, 'I am he!' and, 'The time is at hand!' Do not go after them. 9 And when you hear of wars and tumults, do not be terrified, for these things must first take place, but the end will not be at once."

Jesus Foretells Wars and Persecution

10 Then he said to them, "Nation will rise against nation, and kingdom against kingdom. 11 There will be great earthquakes, and in various places famines and pestilences. And there will be terrors and great signs from heaven. 12 But before all this they will lay their hands on you and persecute you, delivering you up to the synagogues and prisons, and you will be brought before kings and governors for my name's sake. 13 This will be your opportunity to bear witness. 14 Settle it therefore in your minds not to meditate beforehand how to answer, 15 for I will give you a mouth and wisdom, which none of your adversaries will be able to withstand or contradict. 16 You will be delivered up even by parents and brothers and relatives and friends, and some of you they will put to death. 17 You will be hated by all for my name's sake. 18 But not a hair of your head will perish. 19 By your endurance you will gain your lives.

Jesus Foretells Destruction of Jerusalem

20 "But when you see Jerusalem surrounded by armies, then know that its desolation has come near. 21 Then let those who are in Judea flee to the mountains, and let

those who are inside the city depart, and let not those who are out in the country enter it, 22 for these are days of vengeance, to fulfill all that is written. 23 Alas for women who are pregnant and for those who are nursing infants in those days! For there will be great distress upon the earth and wrath against this people. 24 They will fall by the edge of the sword and be led captive among all nations, and Jerusalem will be trampled underfoot by the Gentiles, until the times of the Gentiles are fulfilled.

The Coming of the Son of Man

25 "And there will be signs in sun and moon and stars, and on the earth distress of nations in perplexity because of the roaring of the sea and the waves, 26 people fainting with fear and with foreboding of what is coming on the world. For the powers of the heavens will be shaken. 27 And then they will see the Son of Man coming in a cloud with power and great glory. 28 Now when these things begin to take place, straighten up and raise your heads, because your redemption is drawing near."

The Lesson of the Fig Tree

29 And he told them a parable: "Look at the fig tree, and all the trees. 30 As soon as they come out in leaf, you see for yourselves and know that the summer is already near. 31 So also, when you see these things taking place, you know that the kingdom of God is near. 32 Truly, I say to you, this generation will not pass away until all has taken

place. 33 Heaven and earth will pass away, but my words will not pass away.

Watch Yourselves

34 "But watch yourselves lest your hearts be weighed down with dissipation and drunkenness and cares of this life, and that day come upon you suddenly like a trap. 35 For it will come upon all who dwell on the face of the whole earth. 36 But stay awake at all times, praying that you may have strength to escape all these things that are going to take place, and to stand before the Son of Man."

37 And every day he was teaching in the temple, but at night he went out and lodged on the mount called Olivet. 38 And early in the morning all the people came to him in the temple to hear him.

MONDAY

JOSH SPEARS

It all seems a bit harsh. One (unbelieving) scholar can't reconcile it. One (believing) devotional writer struggles with it too. The Jesus of the Beatitudes seems to be a different Jesus from the Olivet Discourse. "Turn the other cheek" vs. "These are days of vengeance"; "Blessed are the meek" vs. "Power and great glory." But then Jesus does something quite Jesus-like. He pulls them all together with, "Your redemption is drawing near." In what sense does redemption draw near for Christ's disciples? In the destruction of the Temple. That too seems odd. How could the destruction of the Temple be a redemption? Isn't that where God promised to meet his people? Isn't that the place of worship and sacrifice? Indeed. Until Jesus, the True Temple.

The fullness of God, dwelling bodily in Jesus of Nazareth, makes Jesus's body *the* Temple. Consequently, there's no need of another physical Temple. The Old Temple must go. It cannot remain. This is where the Christ of the Beatitudes meets the Christ of the Olivet

Discourse. Because he is the true Temple, the false temple must go, its sacrificial system fulfilled in the One True Sacrifice. This is nothing less than the gracious work of the risen Christ, stripping away the Old Man and uniting us to the New Man. The Earthly Temple must be replaced by the Heavenly Temple. The physical Temple razed to make way for the raised Spiritual (read: Holy Spirit empowered) Temple.

The presence of the triune God resides fully in the resurrected body of the Son. And this we need, to be redeemed from our old ways of sacrifice, our old lives of labor under the curse, our old man. Grace strips us of those structures and strictures. The Spirit who raised up Christ's body, the New Temple, raises us with him, unites us to him and in so doing makes us the New Temple. Christ deals ruthlessly with the Old Man so that I can deal peacefully with the New.

O Lord Jesus Christ, whose bodily Temple was rent on behalf of the world, grant that we may patiently endure the rending of our temples, both the temple of our idolatrous works and the temple or our bodies, that we might be resurrected to new life. This we ask of your Father and by your Spirit with whom you reign over all things. Amen.

TUESDAY

HANNAH BERRETT

I LOVE TALKING ABOUT PERSONALITY TYPES, BUT especially Enneagram types, which focus on what we fear and what drives us. Those discussions tend to punch me in the gut pretty hard.

I'm an Enneagram type 3. I fear, not failure itself, but being *perceived* as a failure. Perception is everything. How I'm viewed by others drives my actions and decisions far more often than I would like to admit. I pretend I understand things I don't. I try to deflect blame when I make mistakes. I lie about my motivations and choices when I think people are going to think poorly of me if I tell them the truth.

Jesus liked to call people out. And when he warns his disciples about the scribes "in the hearing of all the people" he adds an extra layer of sass. He points out how much they show off their holiness in public...while condemning them in public.

And just a few verses earlier, these scribes sent spies to question Jesus. They weren't sincere; they didn't really want to learn from Jesus's teaching. They questioned him in public, but they weren't able to trick him into being duplicitous or inconsistent. And his answers silenced them.

And while Jesus condemns the behavior of the scribes —the behavior that mirrors my own—he extols the behavior of the widow who gives her offering. Unlike the scribes and unlike me, she is sincere, making decisions because she believes they are right, not because she believes they will make her appear the best to others.

Lord, help me cultivate sincerity. I want to make decisions based on my desire to serve you, not because I want people to hold me in high esteem. Help me value your opinion of me over all others. Amen.

WEDNESDAY

KAITLIN MARTIN

HAVE YOU EVER NOTICED THAT WHEN THE
Sadducees and Pharisees try to catch Jesus saying something wrong they ask really interesting questions? Sure,
they might not be the most important questions one could
ask the Son of God, but that doesn't make them uninter-
esting. Their motive is what Jesus comes back to over and
over again. What's behind their questions?

For that matter, what's behind our questions? We all
have them, right? My children love to ask questions, but I
wouldn't consider a lot of them the "big questions." They
ask things like "What color were dinosaurs?" and while I
find dinosaurs fascinating and I'm curious, it's not the
kind of question that keeps me up at night. Those are
questions like when (or if) we'll ever be out of debt or if
we'll stay healthy this month. Sure they are big and
important to me, but I think if Jesus were sitting in front
of me, he'd get to the motivation behind my questions and
worries. And most of the time the answer is that I have a

lot of fear and I don't trust God to take care of me despite how he's done so in the past.

And I think about that every time I hear the story of the widow who offers all she has. How does she have that much trust? It's not like she'll be starting school to learn a new skill for a new career. Jesus says that she's done, at a zero bank account. Who cares for her? And beyond that, does what she gives matter? Those are such big questions and cut us all down to the real question: what is the motive behind our questions?

Jesus, make us a people who look to you to fix our motivations. Open our eyes to our fears, worries, and motives. Help us love you more. Thank you for being gracious and loving us enough to ask about our motives. Thank you for sacrificing your all for us when we thought we had enough already. We are content with the wrong things and don't see what we really need, what we're really asking. Thank you for not putting up with our shallow ways. We need heart changes where you offer life in exchange for death and sin. Help us love you with right motives. Help us live with right motives for your glory. Amen.

THURSDAY

ALISON BUXTON

I was talking with an older family member recently. He was complaining about the homeless panhandling on our city street corners and camping under bridges. "If people would just stop handing them money, they'd quit begging," he said. "It seems like it's always young women in beat up cars, who clearly don't have much themselves, who are giving handouts. I'm sure they have good hearts but I just want to tell them to use their heads."

I didn't say much because this is so familiar to me. In the fundamentalist circles of my youth, we cherry-picked scriptures to justify our financial choices, mostly claiming it was a big sin not to manage our money well and redefining the needle's eye into oblivion. Maybe it's complicated.

But maybe not. As I have gotten older I have noticed something. It's the people on the fringes, the outcasts, the folks excluded from cis-het, patriarchal, white American evangelicalism who astound me with their generosity, love, and welcome... people who would have been the widows, orphans, eunuchs, and lepers of Jesus's day. Jesus always showed up for those folks. He loved, and still loves, the people on the margins. He didn't have much use for the religious types who used scripture to trap, attack, and wound.

Old habits die hard. I'm struggling to walk away from the fight when people whip out the Bible and wield it like a weapon. At the end of the day, I think what really matters is giving up trying to be right and instead doing justice, loving mercy, and walking humbly. It's not easy. But I take comfort in Jesus and the fact that, while the arguments and accusations were flying, he saw the widow in her generous poverty.

Jesus, quash my need to be right. Give me eyes to see where your love is turning poverty into riches and brokenness into beauty all around me.

FRIDAY

JAKE SPENCER

WHEN I WAS A KID, I CONSTANTLY ARGUED WITH MY parents, always attempting to get my way. I am reminded of this unfortunate part of my personality now because I am experiencing these arguments from the other side. The same pleas for a change of heart and the same (seemingly) rock-solid logical proofs that I employed as a child again fail to make much of a difference to the parent. My refusal to change a decision makes my son just as frustrated and angry as I once was. I want to stop the story there and point out that one day my grandchildren will probably argue in vain with their parents and we can have a good laugh about it. But stopping there doesn't tell the entire story.

The truth is, I am still the kid who is arguing, thinking that I understand the truth of a situation better than God my father. I build lengthy mental treatises on why something I want to do should be OK with God or why I am justified in neglecting some good work. Sometimes I even convince myself that I have won the argument and that

God and I are on the same side. But you cannot trick God, convince God, or argue God to your point of view. The scribes and Sadducees thought they could outfox Jesus by using crafty words and rhetoric. They always failed, just as I will always fail when I do not submit in obedience to my heavenly father.

Lord, you know what is best and your ways are perfect. Please grant me a heart that yields to your instruction and does not reason itself into sin. Amen.

SATURDAY

ERIKA FORREST

I'VE ENCOUNTERED THE STORY OF THE GENEROUS widow many times, but a few years ago I listened to a sermon on this passage from a novel perspective, in the context of Luke 20:45–47. Never had I heard the story framed as a poor widow so poorly provided for by the priest that she tosses away her only two small coins out of disappointment and frustration. Never had I heard the story depicted as a priest sitting on a self-righteous throne, begrudgingly giving the widow a few pennies from the temple treasury to silence her begging. Never had I heard the story as a woman giving up and surrendering her life to God because God's people let her down. Never had I heard the story as anything other than a parable about a cheerful giver.

Instead of reading it as Jesus praising the woman, he was condemning the priest, casting judgment on his disregard for the law, which required him to provide for the widow. And if I'm honest with myself, at times I am like this priest. I'd much rather be the reluctant giver not even mentioned in this story, or the rich people, giving out of their wealth. My natural inclination is care for myself and my family first, giving to the widows and orphans from my excess, not my first fruits. My sinful nature wants to hoard away in barns and worry only about me and mine. I want to be seen as generous and helpful, but I don't give out of my desire for the fullness of God's kingdom; I give out of obligation or desire for praise.

But this is not the cheerful giver Jesus wants to see. This is not the holy priesthood to which we are called. This is not the justice with which we are commanded to act, the kindness with which we are commanded to love, the humility in which we are commanded to walk. We are commanded to seek God's kingdom on earth and work towards that reality. Our giving should be out of this desire to love the kingdom completely, not out of obligation or desire for honor. We have to care for the widows and orphans as if they are our own family, because, in fact, they are; they are our brothers and sisters in Christ, and bound to us by the blood of Christ.

Dear Father, grow in me a heart more like yours, that desires to give abundantly to your children, so that no widow has only two coins to give. Strip me of my self-righteousness and sinful desire for honor and recognition. Help to me follow your commandments and help bring your kingdom come.

SUNDAY

REFLECTIONS ON THE LAST WEEK AND THE
RESURRECTION LIFE TO COME

WEEK FOUR

PLOTS & PRAYERS (LUKE 22)

LUKE 22

The Plot to Kill Jesus

22 Now the Feast of Unleavened Bread drew near, which is called the Passover. 2 And the chief priests and the scribes were seeking how to put him to death, for they feared the people.

Judas to Betray Jesus

3 Then Satan entered into Judas called Iscariot, who was of the number of the twelve. 4 He went away and conferred with the chief priests and officers how he might betray him to them. 5 And they were glad, and agreed to give him money. 6 So he consented and sought an opportunity to betray him to them in the absence of a crowd.

The Passover with the Disciples

7 Then came the day of Unleavened Bread, on which the Passover lamb had to be sacrificed. 8 So Jesus sent Peter and John, saying, "Go and prepare the Passover for us, that we may eat it." 9 They said to him, "Where will you have us prepare it?" 10 He said to them, "Behold, when you have entered the city, a man carrying a jar of water will meet you. Follow him into the house that he enters 11 and tell the master of the house, 'The Teacher says to you, Where is the guest room, where I may eat the Passover with my disciples?' 12 And he will show you a large upper room furnished; prepare it there." 13 And they went and found it just as he had told them, and they prepared the Passover.

Institution of the Lord's Supper

14 And when the hour came, he reclined at table, and the apostles with him. 15 And he said to them, "I have earnestly desired to eat this Passover with you before I suffer. 16 For I tell you I will not eat it until it is fulfilled in the kingdom of God." 17 And he took a cup, and when he had given thanks he said, "Take this, and divide it among yourselves. 18 For I tell you that from now on I will not drink of the fruit of the vine until the kingdom of God comes." 19 And he took bread, and when he had given thanks, he broke it and gave it to them, saying, "This is my body, which is given for you. Do this in remembrance of me." 20 And likewise the cup after they had

eaten, saying, "This cup that is poured out for you is the new covenant in my blood. 21 But behold, the hand of him who betrays me is with me on the table. 22 For the Son of Man goes as it has been determined, but woe to that man by whom he is betrayed!" 23 And they began to question one another, which of them it could be who was going to do this.

Who Is the Greatest?

24 A dispute also arose among them, as to which of them was to be regarded as the greatest. 25 And he said to them, "The kings of the Gentiles exercise lordship over them, and those in authority over them are called benefactors. 26 But not so with you. Rather, let the greatest among you become as the youngest, and the leader as one who serves. 27 For who is the greater, one who reclines at table or one who serves? Is it not the one who reclines at table? But I am among you as the one who serves.

28 "You are those who have stayed with me in my trials, 29 and I assign to you, as my Father assigned to me, a kingdom, 30 that you may eat and drink at my table in my kingdom and sit on thrones judging the twelve tribes of Israel.

Jesus Foretells Peter's Denial

31 "Simon, Simon, behold, Satan demanded to have you, [d] that he might sift you like wheat, 32 but I have prayed for you that your faith may not fail. And when you have

turned again, strengthen your brothers." 33 Peter said to him, "Lord, I am ready to go with you both to prison and to death." 34 Jesus said, "I tell you, Peter, the rooster will not crow this day, until you deny three times that you know me."

Scripture Must Be Fulfilled in Jesus

35 And he said to them, "When I sent you out with no moneybag or knapsack or sandals, did you lack anything?" They said, "Nothing." 36 He said to them, "But now let the one who has a moneybag take it, and likewise a knapsack. And let the one who has no sword sell his cloak and buy one. 37 For I tell you that this Scripture must be fulfilled in me: 'And he was numbered with the transgressors.' For what is written about me has its fulfillment." 38 And they said, "Look, Lord, here are two swords." And he said to them, "It is enough."

Jesus Prays on the Mount of Olives

39 And he came out and went, as was his custom, to the Mount of Olives, and the disciples followed him. 40 And when he came to the place, he said to them, "Pray that you may not enter into temptation." 41 And he withdrew from them about a stone's throw, and knelt down and prayed, 42 saying, "Father, if you are willing, remove this cup from me. Nevertheless, not my will, but yours, be done." 43 And there appeared to him an angel from heaven, strengthening him. 44 And being in agony he prayed more earnestly; and his sweat became like great

drops of blood falling down to the ground. 45 And when he rose from prayer, he came to the disciples and found them sleeping for sorrow, 46 and he said to them, "Why are you sleeping? Rise and pray that you may not enter into temptation."

Betrayal and Arrest of Jesus

47 While he was still speaking, there came a crowd, and the man called Judas, one of the twelve, was leading them. He drew near to Jesus to kiss him, 48 but Jesus said to him, "Judas, would you betray the Son of Man with a kiss?" 49 And when those who were around him saw what would follow, they said, "Lord, shall we strike with the sword?" 50 And one of them struck the servant of the high priest and cut off his right ear. 51 But Jesus said, "No more of this!" And he touched his ear and healed him. 52 Then Jesus said to the chief priests and officers of the temple and elders, who had come out against him, "Have you come out as against a robber, with swords and clubs? 53 When I was with you day after day in the temple, you did not lay hands on me. But this is your hour, and the power of darkness."

Peter Denies Jesus

54 Then they seized him and led him away, bringing him into the high priest's house, and Peter was following at a distance. 55 And when they had kindled a fire in the middle of the courtyard and sat down together, Peter sat down among them. 56 Then a servant girl, seeing him as

he sat in the light and looking closely at him, said, "This man also was with him." 57 But he denied it, saying, "Woman, I do not know him." 58 And a little later someone else saw him and said, "You also are one of them." But Peter said, "Man, I am not." 59 And after an interval of about an hour still another insisted, saying, "Certainly this man also was with him, for he too is a Galilean." 60 But Peter said, "Man, I do not know what you are talking about." And immediately, while he was still speaking, the rooster crowed. 61 And the Lord turned and looked at Peter. And Peter remembered the saying of the Lord, how he had said to him, "Before the rooster crows today, you will deny me three times." 62 And he went out and wept bitterly.

Jesus Is Mocked

63 Now the men who were holding Jesus in custody were mocking him as they beat him. 64 They also blindfolded him and kept asking him, "Prophesy! Who is it that struck you?" 65 And they said many other things against him, blaspheming him.

Jesus Before the Council

66 When day came, the assembly of the elders of the people gathered together, both chief priests and scribes. And they led him away to their council, and they said, 67 "If you are the Christ, tell us." But he said to them, "If I tell you, you will not believe, 68 and if I ask you, you will not answer. 69 But from now on the Son of Man shall

be seated at the right hand of the power of God." 70 So they all said, "Are you the Son of God, then?" And he said to them, "You say that I am." 71 Then they said, "What further testimony do we need? We have heard it ourselves from his own lips."

MONDAY

KAITLIN MARTIN

So there's a lot that happens in Luke 22, but I want to focus on verses 39–46 where Jesus is praying on the Mount of Olives and the disciples fall asleep. Prior to this part of the chapter, Jesus predicts his disciples' abandonment, Peter's denial, and Judas's betrayal. So Jesus goes to this place and prays, but first he tells his disciples to "pray that you may not enter into temptation." Jesus has predicted some pretty cruel and hurtful behavior from his closest allies and friends, and their response is to claim that they would never do such things. How often are we like that, rushing quickly to defend ourselves against even hypothetical accusations? And here Jesus is basically telling them to pray so they can avoid temptation, perhaps even to pray and avoid the temptation to betray Jesus and deny him. But they fall asleep. We do that, too, right? Not in the literal sense, but spiritually, like not praying about a decision we need to make because we think we can handle it on our own. And why don't we pray to avoid temptation? Is it because we don't recognize it, like the disciples and their upcoming betrayal? Or because we hold the false view of ourselves that we wouldn't act like that?

The good news is that even though the disciples betrayed Jesus, he died for that moment. He died and carried every temptation you fall into as well, and he did it because he loves you! And he can redeem you from your past, and he can help you see the temptations around you so you might avoid them in the future, too.

Father, Son, and Spirit, give us eyes to see who we really are—what we are really like. Give us eyes to see the temptations we face and fall into. Forgive us for the many times we don't pray and don't see. You died and rose again so that we would have power to stand against temptation, and I ask that we would all seek to love you and keep our eyes on you to avoid temptation when it comes. Thank you for telling us what we are really like. We need the truth in order to change. Thank you for dying for us anyway. You knew they would fail you. You know we fail you, too. But it's not the end of the story, and we are so grateful for that. Help us be honest with ourselves and stand against the temptations we face. Amen

TUESDAY

WES MARTIN

I want what I want. And that's my biggest problem. At worst, I will do whatever it takes to get what I want. Now sometimes maybe it doesn't seem that bad. I want a fifth slice of pizza, I want to watch Netflix rather than do my work or read the Bible. But sometimes I get desperate and I don't want to pray for things, because I'm worried God's answer might be *No* and I'm convinced that, really, I know what's best. So, I'll do things my way without asking God. I'll go ahead and make the unwise choice that I know is probably a bad idea. But I really *need* to have this, I tell myself.

That's the thing, God *always* answers prayer, but often, out of his kindness and love for us, his answer is *No*. So sometimes I don't pray. I'm pretty sure if I had done more praying and waiting I would have made different decisions at times. I'm also certain that I need to learn to trust God more, to stop falling asleep praying (or maybe I should start praying enough that I *could* fall asleep praying), and be willing to say, "God, thank you that I can bring anything I want to you. I want *this*. But not my will, your will be done." Because really, what God wants, what God answers, is what is actually best for me! We can trust him! Jesus was willing to say "Not my will, but yours be done, Father," even knowing that when God answered, it would lead Jesus to the cross for our sins.

Heavenly father, I thank you that we can come with the true desires of our hearts and ask you for things. I thank you that we can trust you so much that however you answer our prayers, yes or no, it truly is for our good. Forgive me for my lack of prayer. Thank you that you don't quit on me when I have quit on you. In Jesus's name, Amen.

WEDNESDAY

BECKY CARLOZZI

When Judas left everything to follow Jesus, he couldn't have possibly imagined that his story would have ended the way it did. Luke 22:3–4 tells us that Satan entered into Judas and then he went away to confer with the chief priests in arguably the most famous betrayal in history. I wonder how this decision materialized in Judas over the course of time. When did he first become discontent with the direction of Jesus's ministry? Did his zeal slowly turn into frustration, bitterness, and resentment? My guess is that the process was rather insidious, despite the act of betrayal, which transpired quite quickly.

Satan is a master at cultivating hatred in our hearts over time. I want to become more aware of the ways he slowly turns my heart against others. Ascribing sinful motives and filling gaps in stories with the worst possible narratives are methods Satan uses in my life. I'm often not even aware of this process occurring until it boils over into something more obvious, like biting sarcasm or disdain.

My lack of awareness is possibly connected to my lack

of belief and sensitivity to the convicting work of the Holy Spirit in my heart. I admit that many days hate seems more powerful than love. The story of Judas's betrayal, as well as my own struggles to love others can feel depressing at times. How grateful I am that Lent is followed by Easter. The church calendar reminds me every year that hatred, death, and the devil do not have the final word. Love is more powerful even when hate feels more familiar.

Lord, I admit that it is way too easy for me to build narratives that conveniently make me the victim and others the villain. I let these thoughts simmer and fester, giving Satan footing to cultivate hatred. I go days without heeding the conviction of the Holy Spirit, who through repentance generates love. I'm asking that you change this narrative and soften my heart to respond to the Spirit's work in my life. Amen.

THURSDAY

MATT TEESELINK

ONE OF THE GREATEST PLOTS OF MY JUNIOR HIGH years came during eighth grade football season. While I went to every practice and wore the pads, the sidelines were my real "game" during the actual game. You can probably still hear the joy exuding from me all these years later. Despite my benchwarmer's enthusiasm, my original plan was to quit the team. I was done standing on the sidelines, watching us lose every game. I was going to tell the coach off, tell him how he didn't care about the team but only cared about winning, and how he wasn't very good at that, either. As I kicked open the big metal locker room door, my plot began to unravel. I kicked the door into my coach, and it left a mark. My coach was hurt on the outside, but he could see I was hurt on the inside. He pulled me aside and promised me playing time (I think I got to play like five plays that season), thus ending my grand plot to quit the team.

In some ways, my plot was like Peter's in Luke 22 when he draws his sword at those who have come to arrest

Jesus. Like Peter, I was angry and vengeful, and I wasn't going to let anyone get in my way. Until they did. At which point I realized that I was small, fallen, and frail. Jesus quickly stops Peter but not before Peter is able to slice off an ear. Peter's plan was not Jesus's plan. Peter's plan was to win the battle with a sword. Jesus's plan was to win the battle with love and sacrifice through the giving of his life.

Jesus, help our plot be your plot. Let us seek your kingdom, your kindness, your compassion, and your forgiveness as we seek to forgive those who have hurt us.

FRIDAY

ALISON BUXTON

THE FLANNEL-BOARD VERSION OF JESUS'S BETRAYAL paints Luke 22 in pretty simple terms: the wicked religious leaders hatched a nasty plot to murder Jesus and Judas was the worst person ever because he helped. At the end of the chapter Jesus prayed for God to make another way, a different plan, but the answer was no.

The problem is, when I read this chapter as an adult, it's not nearly so cut and dried as I remember it. The overall sense I get is one of inevitability. The people, whether it's the Pharisees or Judas or even Jesus, seem like pawns in a way. Yes, there is a plot here, but it's not the one the bad guys came up with: it's God's plot. He came up with this plan. This whole thing is his long-before-creation, perfectly timed and carefully coordinated rescue mission. When Jesus expresses his fear and sweats drops of blood God essentially ignores him. Here is a plot that no prayers will change. An inexorable, nightmarish, redemptive, divine plan.

I'm not sure how I feel about that, honestly. The

scripture says that the adversary entered Judas and he sold Jesus out. Maybe he would have done that anyway, without cosmic intervention. I don't know. What seems clear though, is that he lived long enough to recognize what he had done and he took his own life because of it. He got the bad news: Christ died because of me. But he never got the good news: Christ defeated death for me. And he knew who Jesus was. That is a depth of despair that breaks my heart. For Judas. For every person who doesn't survive the dark night to see the sunrise.

This chapter twists my mind and cows my heart. Here is the terribleness and goodness of God, all wrapped up together. When I get close to this story, God's righteousness seeps through the page and it's too much. The plot was so important that God would deny the prayers of Jesus. For me.

Lord, have mercy. Your ways are mysterious but always good.

SATURDAY

DOUG SERVEN

LUKE 22: 54–62 IS ONE OF THE CITY PRES-IEST passages. It's where we see the symbolism of the rooster in the Scriptures, so it's near and dear to the heart of our church. Roosters are annoying animals. They're symbols of the proud, cocky rulers of the barnyard. They signal their supposed superiority by strutting around, attracting attention, and loudly cockle doodling their message.

Peter can relate. He's been talking smack all along the way. He's bold and brash, saying what he thinks, and leading the pack. He's Jesus's best friend. He's an insider. He's said some amazing things, and he's witnessed even more—he walked on water! He's been in a special seat to see the Kingdom of God in ways no one else has ever witnessed. On this last night at the Last Supper, Jesus tells him what lies ahead. It's a prophecy, one shortly fulfilled. On the same might Judas betrays Jesus for thirty pieces of silver, Jesus tells Peter that he will betray for even less, for basically nothing but to save face in front of people who don't even matter that much. Peter cannot believe it, but Jesus confirms it will be as he says. Jesus doesn't stop him. He doesn't tell him how to prevent it. He lets Peter do it.

We have to trust the Savior in this moment. Jesus isn't preventing every bad thing from taking place. He stewards even our worst moments, and he weaves them into something else, something perhaps better than we expected. Peter betrays not only his best friend, but the Lord and Savior, the Messiah, the King of the Universe, the Lord of Lords and King of Kings, the Alpha and Omega, the one who Was, and Is, and Is to Come. This is how far depravity reaches. It's at this moment that ridiculous cock crows. That signal of pride turns into a call of weakness. Pride turned to humility and even humiliation. Peter wakes up. The darkness has come, but the dawn has come too. There will be a new day, one of grace instead of pride, one of hope instead of despair. Jesus looks at Peter. We're not sure how that happens, but certainly it's the look of love. Of grace. Of forgiveness. Of hope. Of redemption.

Peter can see much more clearly now, and that clarity will develop over time, far more powerfully, and far less annoyingly. The rooster clings to the cross in grace and mercy, in faith and fidelity, in humility and patience. We don't trust in our own power. Nothing in our hands we bring, only to the cross we cling.

Jesus thank you for your clarion call: It's a new day dawning. The darkness will pass. The light will come. Come awake, come awake, Christ has risen from the dead! Help us find ourselves in you. Give us hope in your mercy, even as you lead us through these dark paths. Resurrection is coming!

SUNDAY FEAST DAY

REFLECTIONS ON THE LAST WEEK AND THE RESURRECTION LIFE TO COME

WEEK FIVE

SUPPER & DEATH & RESURRECTION (LUKE 22 & 23)

Jesus Before Pilate

23 THEN THE WHOLE COMPANY OF THEM AROSE AND brought him before Pilate. 2 And they began to accuse him, saying, "We found this man misleading our nation and forbidding us to give tribute to Caesar, and saying that he himself is Christ, a king." 3 And Pilate asked him, "Are you the King of the Jews?" And he answered him, "You have said so." 4 Then Pilate said to the chief priests and the crowds, "I find no guilt in this man." 5 But they were urgent, saying, "He stirs up the people, teaching throughout all Judea, from Galilee even to this place."

Jesus Before Herod

6 When Pilate heard this, he asked whether the man was a Galilean. 7 And when he learned that he belonged to Herod's jurisdiction, he sent him over to Herod, who was himself in Jerusalem at that time. 8 When Herod saw

Jesus, he was very glad, for he had long desired to see him, because he had heard about him, and he was hoping to see some sign done by him. 9 So he questioned him at some length, but he made no answer. 10 The chief priests and the scribes stood by, vehemently accusing him. 11 And Herod with his soldiers treated him with contempt and mocked him. Then, arraying him in splendid clothing, he sent him back to Pilate. 12 And Herod and Pilate became friends with each other that very day, for before this they had been at enmity with each other.

13 Pilate then called together the chief priests and the rulers and the people, 14 and said to them, "You brought me this man as one who was misleading the people. And after examining him before you, behold, I did not find this man guilty of any of your charges against him. 15 Neither did Herod, for he sent him back to us. Look, nothing deserving death has been done by him. 16 I will therefore punish and release him."

Pilate Delivers Jesus to Be Crucified

18 But they all cried out together, "Away with this man, and release to us Barabbas"— 19 a man who had been thrown into prison for an insurrection started in the city and for murder. 20 Pilate addressed them once more, desiring to release Jesus, 21 but they kept shouting, "Crucify, crucify him!" 22 A third time he said to them, "Why? What evil has he done? I have found in him no guilt deserving death. I will therefore punish and release him." 23 But they were urgent, demanding with loud

cries that he should be crucified. And their voices prevailed. 24 So Pilate decided that their demand should be granted. 25 He released the man who had been thrown into prison for insurrection and murder, for whom they asked, but he delivered Jesus over to their will.

The Crucifixion

26 And as they led him away, they seized one Simon of Cyrene, who was coming in from the country, and laid on him the cross, to carry it behind Jesus. 27 And there followed him a great multitude of the people and of women who were mourning and lamenting for him. 28 But turning to them Jesus said, "Daughters of Jerusalem, do not weep for me, but weep for yourselves and for your children. 29 For behold, the days are coming when they will say, 'Blessed are the barren and the wombs that never bore and the breasts that never nursed!' 30 Then they will begin to say to the mountains, 'Fall on us,' and to the hills, 'Cover us.' 31 For if they do these things when the wood is green, what will happen when it is dry?"

32 Two others, who were criminals, were led away to be put to death with him. 33 And when they came to the place that is called The Skull, there they crucified him, and the criminals, one on his right and one on his left. 34 And Jesus said, "Father, forgive them, for they know not what they do." And they cast lots to divide his garments. 35 And the people stood by, watching, but the rulers scoffed at him, saying, "He saved others; let him save himself, if he is the Christ of God, his Chosen One!"

36 The soldiers also mocked him, coming up and offering him sour wine 37 and saying, "If you are the King of the Jews, save yourself!" 38 There was also an inscription over him, "This is the King of the Jews."

39 One of the criminals who were hanged railed at him, saying, "Are you not the Christ? Save yourself and us!" 40 But the other rebuked him, saying, "Do you not fear God, since you are under the same sentence of condemnation? 41 And we indeed justly, for we are receiving the due reward of our deeds; but this man has done nothing wrong." 42 And he said, "Jesus, remember me when you come into your kingdom." 43 And he said to him, "Truly, I say to you, today you will be with me in paradise."

The Death of Jesus

44 It was now about the sixth hour, and there was darkness over the whole land until the ninth hour, 45 while the sun's light failed. And the curtain of the temple was torn in two. 46 Then Jesus, calling out with a loud voice, said, "Father, into your hands I commit my spirit!" And having said this he breathed his last. 47 Now when the centurion saw what had taken place, he praised God, saying, "Certainly this man was innocent!" 48 And all the crowds that had assembled for this spectacle, when they saw what had taken place, returned home beating their breasts. 49 And all his acquaintances and the women who had followed him from Galilee stood at a distance watching these things.

Jesus Is Buried

50 Now there was a man named Joseph, from the Jewish town of Arimathea. He was a member of the council, a good and righteous man, 51 who had not consented to their decision and action; and he was looking for the kingdom of God. 52 This man went to Pilate and asked for the body of Jesus. 53 Then he took it down and wrapped it in a linen shroud and laid him in a tomb cut in stone, where no one had ever yet been laid. 54 It was the day of Preparation, and the Sabbath was beginning. 55 The women who had come with him from Galilee followed and saw the tomb and how his body was laid. 56 Then they returned and prepared spices and ointments.

On the Sabbath they rested according to the commandment.

MONDAY

MATT TEESELINK

SEVERAL MONTHS AGO OUR SIX-MONTH-OLD, JUDE, began joining us at the supper table. Micah, our two-year-old, would not consider coming to the supper table without making sure his baby brother was joining us. Jude had done nothing to earn his place at the table but in Micah's mind, our table was incomplete without him.

This is where we stand as we come forward for the Lord's Supper. We come helpless, unable to earn our place at the table. The disciples missed this important lesson much like we miss it today. Take the preparation for the Passover: Jesus sends two disciples ahead to prepare the meal. They respond, "But where?" Jesus tells them to find the man carrying a jar and follow him. Find a man carrying a jar? Really? That's it? Peter and John are tasked with preparing a room, but again it is Jesus preparing the way. They simply show up.

After supper there is a debate about who is the greatest. Clearly, the disciples don't get it. After following Jesus, listening to his teaching, witnessing the miracles, sharing this final meal, the disciples still miss the point. Greatness in this world would not be found in who they where, or what they had done, but rather in Christ and his redemption. Just like my son Jude had done nothing to earn his spot at our table, but the supper is incomplete without him.

Jesus, we come to you wanting to earn our place at the table; instead let us rest in the truth that we cannot earn our place, let us rest in the finished work of Christ. Amen.

TUESDAY

KEELY STEGER

I don't consider myself a consummate hostess, but I've thrown a dinner party or two in my day. I've hosted friends, family at Thanksgiving and Christmas Eve, and countless birthday parties for my children and their friends. However, I've not served a single meal in the same vein as Jesus's last supper.

> So Jesus sent Peter and John, saying, "Go and prepare the Passover for us, that we may eat it." They said to him, "Where will you have us prepare it?"

I have a very hard time leaving the details up to others, so the fact that the location is unknown even to the guests gives me pause. He leaves the preparation of the meal to his disciples, another aspect I struggle with, that relinquishing of control. While I might ask a friend to bring a salad or wine, I would never ask them to prepare the main course. Jesus does just that. (He obviously has bigger things on his mind.)

Next, Jesus knowingly dines not only with Judas, who will leave the meal early in order to set into motion his betrayal, but also with Peter, who vehemently refuses to believe that he will deny knowing Jesus three times. This is not the type of person I invite to my dinner parties. I tend to invite the people I'm most comfortable with, hoping to keep the awkward silences and the small talk to a minimum. Jesus knows his death is imminent, but his disciples don't. They are arguing with one another about who is the greatest among them.

If I knew I was facing my last meal on earth, I would plan the food down to the last crumb and the last drop. I would surround myself with all of my favorite people and laughter would be the dominant sound. I would abide no negativity and might even demand the praise and words of affirmation of everyone seated at the table with me.

But then, I'm not Jesus. His final supper is yet another picture of the life and ministry he has led. It's selfless and sacrificial and focused on others.

Father, the more I study the life of Jesus, the more I see how unlike him I truly am. Thank you that he is perfect, because I am not. Thank you that his righteousness is counted as my own. Without him, I have no hope. Amen.

WEDNESDAY

MELISSA WHITTAKER

And he said to them, "I have earnestly desired to eat this Passover with you before I suffer." Luke 22:15

As I read this chapter, it was as if this sentence reached out and grabbed me by the collar saying, "Hey, look at me!" Was Jesus saying, "Yes, you need to be at this meal, but I also need you there, too?" I am the needy one. I need to take communion. I need to meet Jesus there and be reminded of his love for me and sink my roots down into the gospel of grace. I am the sinner in need of forgiveness. I am the mortal one who needs to be reminded that Jesus has conquered death. It never occurred to me that there was any sense in which Jesus "needed" me there too.

His last meal was not idyllic. The disciples gossiped among themselves about who the betrayer would be. Then they had an argument about which of them would be the greatest in Jesus's kingdom. They didn't seem to grasp the gravity of Jesus's words about what was to come.

I have often viewed Jesus as just tolerating them, but these were the people with whom he deeply longed to spend his last hours. And if that was the case at that first communion meal, why would it not be true now? Despite their failures and dysfunctions, he loved them and he wanted to be with them. He feels the same way about me. I am looking for Jesus at communion and he is looking for me, too.

Dear Lord, thank you that you are with us always. Help us to feel that reality, to know your love for us, and enable us to love others through the work of your Spirit in us. Amen.

THURSDAY

APRIL SPENCER

Sometimes I'd like to not be a part of my community, instead wishing I could do it alone. Yes, there's a need for healthy boundaries, but more often, my heart just wants to not engage. To push back against the questions, the intimate knowledge of my life, and the burdens of knowing the crud that my friends are going through. To slip in and out of church unseen, take a break from City Groups, and definitely avoid any participation in church ministry. Beautiful service or fun Christmas party? Yes, please! Hard conversation or marriage conference? Ew. No, Thank you.

But even at Jesus's last meal, he wanted his people near him. He "earnestly" desired to share this moment with them, despite their messiness. His close friends did not always make life easier for him. They were flawed. They denied him, betrayed him, and didn't really listen to him at times. But he still wanted them there, by his side, knowing what was coming, to share the meal. He desired to have close relationships, and I should, too.

It's easy to share in the fun times, the night out with friends, the text groups that make me laugh, the weddings, and gathering with each other to worship together, but it's harder to share the moments of hurt and pain that are peppered in between. It's exhausting and hard to get right, but there's beauty there, spurring us on to love and good deeds. I need my community at the table, where Jesus is already waiting.

Jesus, give me an earnest desire to share my life, the good and the difficult, with my friends, my church, and others around me. Help me be willing to do the same for them. It's tiresome and I can't do it alone, and I'm thankful you're already there.

FRIDAY

JOSH SPEARS

EATING BECOMES LOTS OF THINGS FOR LOTS OF people. At its most basic, eating is necessary for our survival. Eating brings enjoyment. Eating often salves broken hearts. Eating confirms covenants. Eating establishes community. We recently had the most gloriously awkward time eating with new neighbors across the street. Rarely, however, does eating connect to suffering, but this seems to be what Jesus says in Luke 22: *"I earnestly desire to eat this Passover meal with you before I suffer."* The journey to Jerusalem was filled with meals but this one is special. A meal shared with closest friends on the eve of Redemption. A meal to fortify for the work ahead. But Christ doesn't keep this meal only for himself, only for his own suffering. He gives it for those who follow him in that suffering.

Repeatedly throughout the Gospel, he's called others to follow him to Jerusalem and repeatedly he's provided food for those who respond to the call. *This* meal is the culmination of that journey of meals but it doesn't end there. Christ continues to feed those who follow. And how we need that food. We must, like those around that table, take up our cross and follow him; as such, we need that same sustenance. Christ continues to feed us who follow him to the cross, strengthening.

We've just moved my grandmother in with my parents. We're having our first dinner together tonight. She won't remember it. We need the baked ziti to get us through the night ahead and to wake in the morning. We need bread and wine, body and blood, to get through the cross ahead and the resurrection on that morning.

O Christ, Who by Thy flesh and blood does feed Thy people, grant that Thy Spirit, through bread and wine, would empower us to suffer for Thy Kingdom's sake, so that we might rise to new life in the Resurrection; through the same Spirit who reigns with Thee and Thy Father, ever one God, world without end. Amen.

SATURDAY

ERIKA FORREST

THE LAST SUPPER WAS MORE THAN JUST A PASSOVER meal. In some ways, it wasn't even a last supper; it was also a first supper. Jesus's Passover meal looks a whole lot like an engagement ceremony, with Jesus offering up his most valuable asset, his very body and blood, as a dowry, proving just how very much he loves his disciples. He promises to return for his bride once the time is appointed and to bring her back to his father's house. And then, he goes away. And his betrothed waits for his return.

Maybe we don't embark on engagements and marriages like this anymore, but we used to. Intentions were proven and promises were made. Couples waited, for an undetermined length of time, for the bridal suite to be ready. And then, with trumpets and pomp, the bridegroom arrived and received his bride. And it all began with a dinner.

Each week, we reenact the Last Supper, where God reminds us of the promises he made to us at the first supper and we renew our commitment to our groom. We eat the bread and drink the wine, accepting his offer to us and reaffirming our betrothal, knowing that he would and *has* given his very life for our own. This is not just a meal. This is a ceremony. This is a promise. This is an agreement. This is a commitment.

Every week, Jesus proposes to me. Every week, he displays just how much he values me, offering me his body and blood. Every week, he promises he will return for me once the newlywed suite is ready. Every week, he asks for my hand. Every week, I accept his proposal.

Dear Lord, thank you for seeking me as your bride, choosing me as a member of your people. Thank you for loving me so deeply that you died for me, making a way for me to join you in your father's house. Teach me to love you with the same commitment, as you remind me every week that you will return for me.

WEEK SIX

SENTENCING (LUKE 22 & 23)

LUKE 23

Jesus Before Pilate

23 THEN THE WHOLE COMPANY OF THEM AROSE AND brought him before Pilate. 2 And they began to accuse him, saying, "We found this man misleading our nation and forbidding us to give tribute to Caesar, and saying that he himself is Christ, a king." 3 And Pilate asked him, "Are you the King of the Jews?" And he answered him, "You have said so." 4 Then Pilate said to the chief priests and the crowds, "I find no guilt in this man." 5 But they were urgent, saying, "He stirs up the people, teaching throughout all Judea, from Galilee even to this place."

Jesus Before Herod

6 When Pilate heard this, he asked whether the man was a Galilean. 7 And when he learned that he belonged to Herod's jurisdiction, he sent him over to Herod, who was himself in Jerusalem at that time. 8 When Herod saw

Jesus, he was very glad, for he had long desired to see him, because he had heard about him, and he was hoping to see some sign done by him. 9 So he questioned him at some length, but he made no answer. 10 The chief priests and the scribes stood by, vehemently accusing him. 11 And Herod with his soldiers treated him with contempt and mocked him. Then, arraying him in splendid clothing, he sent him back to Pilate. 12 And Herod and Pilate became friends with each other that very day, for before this they had been at enmity with each other.

13 Pilate then called together the chief priests and the rulers and the people, 14 and said to them, "You brought me this man as one who was misleading the people. And after examining him before you, behold, I did not find this man guilty of any of your charges against him. 15 Neither did Herod, for he sent him back to us. Look, nothing deserving death has been done by him. 16 I will therefore punish and release him."

Pilate Delivers Jesus to Be Crucified

18 But they all cried out together, "Away with this man, and release to us Barabbas"— 19 a man who had been thrown into prison for an insurrection started in the city and for murder. 20 Pilate addressed them once more, desiring to release Jesus, 21 but they kept shouting, "Crucify, crucify him!" 22 A third time he said to them, "Why? What evil has he done? I have found in him no guilt deserving death. I will therefore punish and release him." 23 But they were urgent, demanding with loud

cries that he should be crucified. And their voices prevailed. 24 So Pilate decided that their demand should be granted. 25 He released the man who had been thrown into prison for insurrection and murder, for whom they asked, but he delivered Jesus over to their will.

The Crucifixion

26 And as they led him away, they seized one Simon of Cyrene, who was coming in from the country, and laid on him the cross, to carry it behind Jesus. 27 And there followed him a great multitude of the people and of women who were mourning and lamenting for him. 28 But turning to them Jesus said, "Daughters of Jerusalem, do not weep for me, but weep for yourselves and for your children. 29 For behold, the days are coming when they will say, 'Blessed are the barren and the wombs that never bore and the breasts that never nursed!' 30 Then they will begin to say to the mountains, 'Fall on us,' and to the hills, 'Cover us.' 31 For if they do these things when the wood is green, what will happen when it is dry?"

32 Two others, who were criminals, were led away to be put to death with him. 33 And when they came to the place that is called The Skull, there they crucified him, and the criminals, one on his right and one on his left. 34 And Jesus said, "Father, forgive them, for they know not what they do." And they cast lots to divide his garments. 35 And the people stood by, watching, but the rulers scoffed at him, saying, "He saved others; let him save himself, if he is the Christ of God, his Chosen One!"

36 The soldiers also mocked him, coming up and offering him sour wine 37 and saying, "If you are the King of the Jews, save yourself!" 38 There was also an inscription over him, "This is the King of the Jews."

39 One of the criminals who were hanged railed at him, saying, "Are you not the Christ? Save yourself and us!" 40 But the other rebuked him, saying, "Do you not fear God, since you are under the same sentence of condemnation? 41 And we indeed justly, for we are receiving the due reward of our deeds; but this man has done nothing wrong." 42 And he said, "Jesus, remember me when you come into your kingdom." 43 And he said to him, "Truly, I say to you, today you will be with me in paradise."

The Death of Jesus

44 It was now about the sixth hour, and there was darkness over the whole land until the ninth hour, 45 while the sun's light failed. And the curtain of the temple was torn in two. 46 Then Jesus, calling out with a loud voice, said, "Father, into your hands I commit my spirit!" And having said this he breathed his last. 47 Now when the centurion saw what had taken place, he praised God, saying, "Certainly this man was innocent!" 48 And all the crowds that had assembled for this spectacle, when they saw what had taken place, returned home beating their breasts. 49 And all his acquaintances and the women who had followed him from Galilee stood at a distance watching these things.

Jesus Is Buried

50 Now there was a man named Joseph, from the Jewish town of Arimathea. He was a member of the council, a good and righteous man, 51 who had not consented to their decision and action; and he was looking for the kingdom of God. 52 This man went to Pilate and asked for the body of Jesus. 53 Then he took it down and wrapped it in a linen shroud and laid him in a tomb cut in stone, where no one had ever yet been laid. 54 It was the day of Preparation, and the Sabbath was beginning. 55 The women who had come with him from Galilee followed and saw the tomb and how his body was laid. 56 Then they returned and prepared spices and ointments.

On the Sabbath they rested according to the commandment.

MONDAY

HANNAH BERRETT

A CROWD OF PEOPLE CAN BE A TERRIFYING THING.

Peter succumbs to this fear when he betrays Jesus, not wanting to face the wrath of the people who had turned against his teacher.

In a single chapter, the chief priests and the scribes go from fearing the peoples' enthusiasm for Jesus to utilizing the same power of the crowd to accomplish their goal of killing him. At the beginning of chapter: 22, *they are plotting in the shadows, paying Judas to betray Jesus "in the absence of a crowd." But halfway through chapter 23, the people "all cried out together" for Jesus to be put to death, "And their voices prevailed."*

None of the authorities passing Jesus back and forth among themselves wanted to be the responsible party for determining his sentence; that would have meant answering to the crowd. Instead, they turned the decision over to the crowd.

It would be easy for me to spend time contemplating when I have been in fear of a crowd and made decisions out of that fear. But I think I should instead consider when I've been a part of the crowd. When have I been so easily swayed? When have I been so quick to join others in condemnation of someone or something? And what does that fickleness say about how sincerely I believe what I claim to believe? How can I cultivate a faith that stands up against changing tides of public opinion?

Lord, give me patience to develop a faith that cannot be shaken. Help me lay each brick upon my foundation with confidence in its truth and immutability so that it will not fall when opposed.

TUESDAY

KEELY STEGER

And the Lord turned and looked at Peter. And Peter remembered the saying of the Lord, how he had said to him, "Before the rooster crows today, you will deny me three times."

Luke 22:61

I DON'T KNOW HOW YOU FEEL ABOUT THE MOVIE, *THE Passion of the Christ*, but for our family, it's become tradition to watch it each year around this time. It's graphic at times, (and we spare our youngest children some of those scenes) especially as Christ is beaten and crucified. Those scenes cause a visceral reaction in me, and as someone who can be pretty stoic most of the time, anything that provokes such strong emotion is noteworthy.

One of the most haunting scenes takes place during the overnight, illegal "trial" of Christ. As Christ is being questioned and mocked and accused, Peter stands off to the side, being recognized and called out and... denying. When he utters for the third and final time that he doesn't know Jesus, the rooster crows and Jesus turns and catches Peter's eye.

Talk about a visceral reaction. The pain and utter sadness that pass in that moment are truly hard to watch.

Christ knew it was coming; Peter was warned but refused to believe it. Destined to face the ultimate denial, as God would soon turn his back on him as well, Jesus stands utterly alone in his hour of need.

I will watch the movie again in the next week or so, and I will allow my heart to be broken by the story once more. This painful, gut-wrenching story without which I have no hope.

Jesus, thank you never seems to say enough. "Take my life and let me be, consecrated Lord, to thee."

WEDNESDAY

MATT TEESELINK

An insurrectionist and a murderer.

That is who the angry crowd chose to release over Jesus. Luke 23:18-25 tells of the scene of Pilate coming to the crowd to chose between Barabbas and Jesus. The crowd was united in its angry calls for Jesus to be crucified and Barabbas to be released.

We can look at this interaction between Pilate and the crowd and be frustrated by the injustice: Where is the due process? How is this fair? But that is the very thing about Jesus and his coming to earth. The incarnation was not fair. Jesus left his heavenly throne to be met with cheers of "Crucify him!" The crowd chose a murderer to live and Jesus to die.

The reality is that Jesus's sentencing was unjust. The screaming crowd got it wrong, sending an innocent man to his death and setting a guilty man free. This is the story of Christ and his coming to die for sinners like you and me. Christ's judgment was our judgment; he was sentenced to death for our transgressions. When we look at this chapter from Luke we can see the injustice but we should also rest in the knowledge that Christ was willing to take on such injustice in order to redeem us.

Dear Jesus, as we reflect on your sentencing we see the injustice but we are grateful for your sacrifice, dying in our place to redeem us before the Father.

THURSDAY

JAKE SPENCER

WHEN I READ THE BIBLE, SOMETIMES IT'S HARD FOR me to identify with a character and think "That's what I'm like." I know I'm not Jesus! There is no situation where I see myself fighting a giant (or even a regular-sized person) with a slingshot, so I'm not David either. I do see some parallels with the Jacob from the Old Testament—we both do things we know we shouldn't, and God seems to keep loving us anyway.

Here, soon after Jesus is crucified, I find someone what maybe sounds like me: Joseph of Arimathea, "a good and righteous man." Am I a good and righteous man? Most of the time, I want to be. John says that Joseph was a secret disciple of Jesus "for fear of the Jews." That sounds like me! I want everyone to get along, I don't want to rock the boat, and all too often I am content to be too quiet about the faith that burns within me. Mark tells us that when Jesus died, Joseph "took courage" and asked Pilate for Jesus's body. Sometimes I do take courage, and sometimes I rock the boat.

What I most identify with about Joseph is that "he was looking for the kingdom of God." I may not be the kind of person that will take on a giant with a handful of rocks, but for as long as I can remember, I've been looking for the kingdom. I have found that kingdom through faith in Christ. I've had that faith for a long time, but I have not yet been changed into a perfect citizen of that place. As I grow in faith, I learn more of what it means to be a citizen and when I act like a citizen, I become more of one. Like Joseph of Arimathea, I take courage and keep looking for the kingdom.

Lord, thank you for inviting me to join your kingdom. Lead me to a more perfect understanding of what that kingdom looks like and to find more and more of it. Amen.

FRIDAY

DOUG SERVEN

Are you the king of the Jews?

JESUS WAS NOT WHAT THEY WANTED, EVEN THOUGH he was what they needed. They wanted strength, power, justice, wisdom, and might. Jesus was all of those things, but not in the way they expected. They wanted Jesus to drive the Romans out of their lands, and restore their kingdom of glory.

Instead, Jesus ate with sinners. He healed those who were sick. He raised people from the dead. He had friends who were prostitutes and tax collectors. He hardly ever hung out with the people in power. He virtually ignored the players who could have crowned him king. When he did speak to them (namely the scribes and Pharisees), they were furious with what he said and did.

The Jews were not authorized to kill Jesus. They needed the very Romans they hated to do the deed, so they trumped up charges to make it sound like Jesus was a threat to them. He was tried for sedition and treason, for teaching that it was forbidden to give tribute to Caesar, which wasn't true. And besides—they hated giving tribute to Caesar.

Not guilty. But they were urgent. *Are you the king of the Jews? You have said so.* Yes. Yes, he is. We serve this king in this kingdom with his values at his command.

Jesus, thank you for being the king we need, rather than the king we want you to be. Forgive us for failing to recognize you and for failing to live as those who belong to your kingdom. Amen.

SATURDAY

BOBBY GRIFFITH

In December I received a ticket because my headlights were not on; the sun was still out. I took a picture of the sky and thought that was what I could show the judge. I did not realize that it is actually cheaper to pay the ticket than plead "not guilty" and win, due to court costs. Needless to say, a text message from an attorney friend came at just the right moment for me to plead "no contest" and save $500 even though I believe I would have been absolved. We all have moments in our lives where we perceive injustice. These can be small or large. We might know someone who was wronged and feel there is no way to absolve the situation. We live in a culture where connected people commit crimes and seemingly weasel their way out. We see injustice and echo the scriptures by asking "how long?"

Luke's narrative of Christ's trial is maddening. He is clearly innocent. It is a setup with jealousy and high drama. Dozens, if not hundreds, are complicit in this cosmic injustice. It does not feel like the triumphal king or how we might want to bring redemption into the world. Really, it is the hopelessness of the situation that we can find relatable. We have been there. We might be there now. We see it. And the beauty of it is the God who brings hope has been in the most hopeless of situations for us. He experienced injustice. He experienced betrayal. He was victim to a corrupt system. And in the moments we are there, so is he.

Lord, in my moments where all seems lost, and I am abandoned, fill me with comfort, strengthen my faith, and carry me through the valley of the shadow of death. Amen.

PALM SUNDAY FEAST DAY

REFLECTIONS ON THE LAST WEEK AND THE RESURRECTION LIFE TO COME

WEEK SEVEN

PALM SUNDAY & GOOD FRIDAY (LUKE 19 & 23)

LUKE 19

Jesus and Zacchaeus

19 HE ENTERED JERICHO AND WAS PASSING THROUGH.
2 And behold, there was a man named Zacchaeus. He
was a chief tax collector and was rich. 3 And he was
seeking to see who Jesus was, but on account of the crowd
he could not, because he was small in stature. 4 So he ran
on ahead and climbed up into a sycamore tree to see him,
for he was about to pass that way. 5 And when Jesus came
to the place, he looked up and said to him, "Zacchaeus,
hurry and come down, for I must stay at your house
today." 6 So he hurried and came down and received him
joyfully. 7 And when they saw it, they all grumbled, "He
has gone in to be the guest of a man who is a sinner."
8 And Zacchaeus stood and said to the Lord, "Behold,
Lord, the half of my goods I give to the poor. And if I have
defrauded anyone of anything, I restore it fourfold."
9 And Jesus said to him, "Today salvation has come to this

house, since he also is a son of Abraham. 10 For the Son of Man came to seek and to save the lost."

The Parable of the Ten Minas

11 As they heard these things, he proceeded to tell a parable, because he was near to Jerusalem, and because they supposed that the kingdom of God was to appear immediately. 12 He said therefore, "A nobleman went into a far country to receive for himself a kingdom and then return. 13 Calling ten of his servants, he gave them ten minas, and said to them, 'Engage in business until I come.' 14 But his citizens hated him and sent a delegation after him, saying, 'We do not want this man to reign over us.' 15 When he returned, having received the kingdom, he ordered these servants to whom he had given the money to be called to him, that he might know what they had gained by doing business. 16 The first came before him, saying, 'Lord, your mina has made ten minas more.' 17 And he said to him, 'Well done, good servant! Because you have been faithful in a very little, you shall have authority over ten cities.' 18 And the second came, saying, 'Lord, your mina has made five minas.' 19 And he said to him, 'And you are to be over five cities.' 20 Then another came, saying, 'Lord, here is your mina, which I kept laid away in a handkerchief; 21 for I was afraid of you, because you are a severe man. You take what you did not deposit, and reap what you did not sow.' 22 He said to him, 'I will condemn you with your own words, you wicked servant! You knew that I was a severe man, taking what I did not deposit and reaping what I did not sow?

23 Why then did you not put my money in the bank, and at my coming I might have collected it with interest?' 24 And he said to those who stood by, 'Take the mina from him, and give it to the one who has the ten minas.' 25 And they said to him, 'Lord, he has ten minas!' 26 'I tell you that to everyone who has, more will be given, but from the one who has not, even what he has will be taken away. 27 But as for these enemies of mine, who did not want me to reign over them, bring them here and slaughter them before me.'"

The Triumphal Entry

28 And when he had said these things, he went on ahead, going up to Jerusalem. 29 When he drew near to Bethphage and Bethany, at the mount that is called Olivet, he sent two of the disciples, 30 saying, "Go into the village in front of you, where on entering you will find a colt tied, on which no one has ever yet sat. Untie it and bring it here. 31 If anyone asks you, 'Why are you untying it?' you shall say this: 'The Lord has need of it.'" 32 So those who were sent went away and found it just as he had told them. 33 And as they were untying the colt, its owners said to them, "Why are you untying the colt?" 34 And they said, "The Lord has need of it." 35 And they brought it to Jesus, and throwing their cloaks on the colt, they set Jesus on it. 36 And as he rode along, they spread their cloaks on the road. 37 As he was drawing near—already on the way down the Mount of Olives—the whole multitude of his disciples began to rejoice and praise God with a loud voice for all the mighty works that they had seen,

38 saying, "Blessed is the King who comes in the name of the Lord! Peace in heaven and glory in the highest!" 39 And some of the Pharisees in the crowd said to him, "Teacher, rebuke your disciples." 40 He answered, "I tell you, if these were silent, the very stones would cry out."

Jesus Weeps over Jerusalem

41 And when he drew near and saw the city, he wept over it, 42 saying, "Would that you, even you, had known on this day the things that make for peace! But now they are hidden from your eyes. 43 For the days will come upon you, when your enemies will set up a barricade around you and surround you and hem you in on every side 44 and tear you down to the ground, you and your children within you. And they will not leave one stone upon another in you, because you did not know the time of your visitation."

Jesus Cleanses the Temple

45 And he entered the temple and began to drive out those who sold, 46 saying to them, "It is written, 'My house shall be a house of prayer,' but you have made it a den of robbers."

47 And he was teaching daily in the temple. The chief priests and the scribes and the principal men of the people were seeking to destroy him, 48 but they did not find anything they could do, for all the people were hanging on his words.

MONDAY OF HOLY WEEK

ALLISON BROWN

PALM SUNDAY ALWAYS FEELS A LITTLE STRANGE TO me. I wave my palm frond obediently, even joyfully, but, as I read the story of the triumphal entry, I know what's coming. A few days later, the crowd will turn on him. A few days later, and Jesus will be nailed to the cross. The deafening praise, *"Blessed is the King who comes in the name of the Lord! Peace in heaven and glory in the highest!"* so quickly turn into demands to *"Crucify him!"* and jeers of *"If you are the King of the Jews, save yourself!"*

How often the whims of the crowd are reflected in my own heart. My earnest worship on Sunday contrasts with my cynical despair on Monday. My prayers of thanks turn into rants of disappointment, anger, and entitlement. My pleas for justice are deafened by my apathy and self-righteousness. Glory given to God is grabbed back selfishly for my gain. My commitments to action fade away as I scroll through my Twitter feed. My claims of "Jesus is King" are undermined by my loyalty to my empire, my job, and my ambitions.

But just as death on a cross was not Jesus's end, my sin, apathy, and pride are not my end. I am forgiven and redeemed. Because, just seven days later, Jesus will rise again.

Heavenly Father, mercifully grant that we, walking in the way of the cross, may find it none other than the way of life and peace; through Jesus Christ, your Son, our Lord.

TUESDAY OF HOLY WEEK

CATIE FORESTER

JESUS'S TRIUMPHAL ENTRY INTO JERUSALEM CALLS TO mind the C.S. Lewis quote about the child happy to keep making mud pies because he's never heard of the ocean. He doesn't know any better. Of this, Lewis says, "We are far too easily pleased." The people waving palms and celebrating Jesus's arrival, like the ignorant child, have no concept for the kind of savior Jesus is and will prove himself to be. All they know is what they can imagine, and it turns out Jesus is not what they had imagined. He's better, but they don't see that yet. And come Friday it's going to appear that he's in fact the opposite of the conquering hero they had been awaiting, but they don't know what's going to happen on Sunday. It's dramatic irony. Reading Luke 19, I know what's coming in chapter 24: Resurrection. The best news ever, anywhere, for all time. But they're still in the dark.

I know the end of the story, but I don't live like it. I get caught up in the day-to-day drudgery of making metaphorical mud pies and I forget about the beach vacation to the point where it may as well not even exist. It's a humbling realization. It would be way easier to pile on the people who hail Jesus on Sunday and crucify him on Friday. But I have information they don't, information that should make a difference in the way I exist in the world. It's a helpful realization. Because the happy ending is true and it's not too late for me to start living like it.

Thank you, Lord, for creating an end to your story that is far better beyond anything I could ever have imagined. Thank you for redeeming me to be a part of your amazing story. Help me so to live that others would want to be a part of it as well. Amen.

WEDNESDAY OF HOLY WEEK

WES MARTIN

Believing in Jesus is weird. Christians think that we have a king, belong to a kingdom that is not of this world (John 18:36), and are created to praise and bring glory to someone beside ourselves. That goes against everything I was told growing up. I grew up thinking I was my own final authority, belonged to whatever group I decided to join, and that life was about getting the most happiness, the most praise for myself, and having the best for myself. Those were my ambitions and goals as a young man.

Enter Jesus.

Jesus challenged me to move out of the world's call to self-centeredness and move into God's call to Jesus-centeredness. This seems weird, but it's what the world was created for and how our lives truly work best. And it's where real eternal happiness is truly found.

All this happens when we realize that our king is a weird king. He's not an egomaniac vying for power and throwing temper tantrums when people criticize him.

Jesus is the humble king, who comes riding on a donkey. This is the humble way. This is the way that says he comes proclaiming peace. Jesus brings forgiveness for the self-centeredness that sadly still pervades our lives. But he also comes and calls me out of myself to praise him and serve others. The more we realize Jesus is a humble king, *our* humble king, the more we are enabled to rest in him and serve others instead of ourselves. Becoming Jesus-centered saves me from being self-centered.

Jesus, I thank you that you are king. I thank you that even though you are the king of the universe you care about my life. I thank you that you are involved, through your Holy Spirit living in me, in all that I do. And I ask you to draw me to rest in your love, draw my eyes and my mind to think of you so that I might serve you and others better. Help me escape my constant discontent with myself and instead lead me to rest in being yours, in having you as the lover of my soul. Save me from my sin and save me from myself. I ask these things in your Holy Name, the Name by which salvation comes. Amen.

THURSDAY OF HOLY WEEK

JOSH SPEARS

I love Christmas. Love it. Love. It. Even the saccharine cultural mush of it. The real tree, the light stringing, the waiting until the first Sunday of Advent for Sufjan Stevens's five-disc Christmas album. The build up to Christmas day, the obnoxious commercials (and their attendant commercialization of Christmas, sure), all of it. Culturally, the most depressing day of the year for me is the day after Christmas. Walking into stores to see barren walls devoid of Christmas (and already filled with the pink hues of Valentine's Day—ugh!). We practice keeping Christmas until Epiphany, in part to extend my love of Christmas, in part to celebrate Christmastide with the ancient church. Personally, pulling down Christmas at the house the night of Epiphany is equally depressing.

I've acutely felt this for years, but it was only this year that I finally realized why. It's the church calendar. Living out the church calendar each year forces us to move through the life of Christ. It doesn't let us stop at any one point. It moves inexorably, incessantly. I want to camp, like Peter at the Transfiguration on the mount, in the light and glory and pageantry of Christmas. That's, after all, what Christ is. Light. Glory. Freedom. Hope. But the church calendar bites hardest here. I can't stay at Christmas, time moves us resolutely to Lent and then Holy Week and then Maundy Thursday and then Good Friday. Christmas Day must lead to Good Friday. Birth must lead to death and I don't want to die. I want all the glory and light without the humility and dark. Life without Death. Resurrection without Cross. But Luke's Jesus, while born to angels rending the heavens with Glory and promises of peace, spilling that Other World into ours, sets his face toward Jerusalem to die. And so must we.

Almighty and Everliving God, whose Son set his face toward Jerusalem to die on behalf of the world, grant us, by Thy Spirit, to follow Him in the same way that we might be raised to new life both here and in the life to come. Through Him who reigns over all things with you and the Holy Spirit, ever one God, world without end. Amen.

LUKE 23—THE CRUCIFIXION

The Crucifixion

26 And as they led him away, they seized one Simon of Cyrene, who was coming in from the country, and laid on him the cross, to carry it behind Jesus. 27 And there followed him a great multitude of the people and of women who were mourning and lamenting for him. 28 But turning to them Jesus said, "Daughters of Jerusalem, do not weep for me, but weep for yourselves and for your children. 29 For behold, the days are coming when they will say, 'Blessed are the barren and the wombs that never bore and the breasts that never nursed!' 30 Then they will begin to say to the mountains, 'Fall on us,' and to the hills, 'Cover us.' 31 For if they do these things when the wood is green, what will happen when it is dry?"

32 Two others, who were criminals, were led away to be put to death with him. 33 And when they came to the place that is called The Skull, there they crucified him,

and the criminals, one on his right and one on his left. 34 And Jesus said, "Father, forgive them, for they know not what they do." And they cast lots to divide his garments. 35 And the people stood by, watching, but the rulers scoffed at him, saying, "He saved others; let him save himself, if he is the Christ of God, his Chosen One!" 36 The soldiers also mocked him, coming up and offering him sour wine 37 and saying, "If you are the King of the Jews, save yourself!" 38 There was also an inscription over him, "This is the King of the Jews."

39 One of the criminals who were hanged railed at him, saying, "Are you not the Christ? Save yourself and us!" 40 But the other rebuked him, saying, "Do you not fear God, since you are under the same sentence of condemnation? 41 And we indeed justly, for we are receiving the due reward of our deeds; but this man has done nothing wrong." 42 And he said, "Jesus, remember me when you come into your kingdom." 43 And he said to him, "Truly, I say to you, today you will be with me in paradise."

The Death of Jesus

44 It was now about the sixth hour, and there was darkness over the whole land until the ninth hour, 45 while the sun's light failed. And the curtain of the temple was torn in two. 46 Then Jesus, calling out with a loud voice, said, "Father, into your hands I commit my spirit!" And having said this he breathed his last. 47 Now when the centurion saw what had taken place, he praised God, saying, "Certainly this man was innocent!" 48 And all the

crowds that had assembled for this spectacle, when they saw what had taken place, returned home beating their breasts. 49 And all his acquaintances and the women who had followed him from Galilee stood at a distance watching these things.

Jesus Is Buried

50 Now there was a man named Joseph, from the Jewish town of Arimathea. He was a member of the council, a good and righteous man, 51 who had not consented to their decision and action; and he was looking for the kingdom of God. 52 This man went to Pilate and asked for the body of Jesus. 53 Then he took it down and wrapped it in a linen shroud and laid him in a tomb cut in stone, where no one had ever yet been laid. 54 It was the day of Preparation, and the Sabbath was beginning. 55 The women who had come with him from Galilee followed and saw the tomb and how his body was laid. 56 Then they returned and prepared spices and ointments.

On the Sabbath they rested according to the commandment.

GOOD FRIDAY

BECKY CARLOZZI

The last words of Jesus before he died were, *"Father, into your hands I commit my spirit"* (Luke 23:46). Psalm 31:5 says, *"Into your hands I commit my spirit; redeem me, O Lord, the God of truth."* By quoting from this verse, Jesus is calling on the very nature of his Father ("the God of truth") to complete the Triune God's plan of redemption through sacrificial love. By the redemption of the Son and the gift of the Spirit, all of creation is being redeemed.

Truth and sacrifice are the same ingredients present when I've witnessed manifestations of God's kingdom on earth today. When truth is spoken without a willingness to sacrifice, the sentiment is often harsh and damning. Sacrifice without truth is empty, foolish, and self-serving. However, when truth and sacrifice walk hand in hand, love is present, true community is possible, and redemption permeates.

The obstacle to both truth and sacrifice is the same: me. Truth doesn't always make me look good so I'd rather avoid it. Sacrifice demands that I die to my need to be right, not to mention my need for comfort and status, which feels impossible most days.

I need to be reminded that we are not left helpless and hopeless. When Jesus relinquished his spirit into his Father's hands, he shared that Spirit back with his people. John 16:7 says, *"Nevertheless, I tell you the truth: it is to your advantage that I go away, for if I do not go away, the Helper will not come to you. But if I go, I will send him to you."* Because of Christ's sacrifice, we have the necessary ingredient inside us, the Holy Spirit, who in the very nature of the Trinity, radiates redemption wherever present.

Father, Son and Holy Spirit, thank you for promising to change us. Convict us in the areas where we are resistant to your redeeming work. Increase our faith so that we can love others fully, in a manner reflective of the Trinity.

GOOD FRIDAY SERVICE

Good Friday is a solemn day to remember the sacrifice of Jesus Christ on the cross. We remember our own sins, but also the suffering God who died to atone for them. Historically, Christians have observed this day with a somber tone.. Please enter and exit the sanctuary in silence.

Opening Prayer

Let us pray.
Almighty God, we pray you graciously to behold this your family, for whom our Lord Jesus Christ was willing to be betrayed, and given into the hands of sinners, and to suffer death upon the cross; who now lives and reigns with you and the Holy Spirit, one God, for ever and ever. *Amen.*

Old Testament Reading

Behold, my servant shall act wisely; he shall be high and lifted up, and shall be exalted. As many were astonished at you—his appearance was so marred, beyond human semblance, and his form beyond that of the children of mankind—so shall he sprinkle many nations; kings shall shut their mouths because of him; for that which has not been told them they see, and that which they have not heard they understand.

Who has believed what he has heard from us? And to whom has the arm of the LORD been revealed? For he grew up before him like a young plant, and like a root out of dry ground; he had no form or majesty that we should look at him, and no beauty that we should desire him. He was despised and rejected by men; a man of sorrows, and acquainted with grief; and as one from whom men hide their faces he was despised, and we esteemed him not. Surely he has borne our griefs and carried our sorrows; yet we esteemed him stricken, smitten by God, and afflicted. But he was pierced for our transgressions; he was crushed for our iniquities upon him was the chastisement that brought us peace, and with his wounds we are healed. All we like sheep have gone astray; we have turned—every one—to his own way; and the LORD has laid on him the iniquity of us all. He was oppressed, and he was afflicted, yet he opened not his mouth; like a lamb that is led to the slaughter, and like a sheep that before its shearers is silent, so he opened not his mouth. By oppression and judgment he was taken away; and as for his generation, who considered that he was cut off out of the land of the living, stricken for the transgression of my people? And they made his grave with the wicked and with a rich man in his death, although he had done no violence, and there was no deceit in his mouth. Yet it was the will of the LORD to crush him; he has put him to grief; when his soul makes an offering for guilt, he shall see his offspring; he shall prolong his days; the will of the LORD shall prosper in his hand. Out of the anguish of his soul he shall see and be satisfied; by his knowledge shall the righteous one, my servant, make many to be accounted righteous, and he shall bear their iniquities. Therefore I will divide him a portion with the many, and he shall divide the spoil with the strong, because he poured out his soul to death and was numbered with the transgressors yet he bore the sin of many, and makes intercession for the transgressors. *Isaiah 52:13–53:12*

Psalter Reading

My God, my God, why have you forsaken me? Why are you so far from saving me, from the words of my groaning? O my God, I cry by day, but you do not answer, and by night, but I find no rest. Yet you are holy, enthroned on the praises of Israel. In you our fathers trusted; they trusted, and you delivered them.To you they cried and were rescued; in you they trusted and were not put to shame. But I am a worm and not a man, scorned by mankind and despised by the people. All who see me mock me; they make mouths at me; they wag their heads;

He trusts in the LORD; let him deliver him; let him rescue him, for he delights in him! Yet you are he who took me from the womb; you made me trust you at my mother's breasts. On you was I cast from my birth, and from my mother's womb you have been my God. Be not far from me, for trouble is near, and there is none to help. *Psalm 22:1–11*

Who is This So Weak and Helpless? William How, 1867

1. Who is this, so weak and helpless,
   Child of lowly Hebrew maid,
   Rudely in a stable sheltered,
   Coldly in a manger laid?
   'Tis the Lord of all creation,
   Who this wondrous path has trod;
   He is Lord from everlasting,
   And to everlasting God.

2. Who is this, a Man of Sorrows,
   Walking sadly life's hard way,
   Homeless, weary, sighing,
   weeping over sin and Satan's sway?
   Tis our God, our glorious Savior,
   who above the starry sky
   Is for us a place preparing,
   where no tear can dim the eye.

3. Who is this? Behold him
   shedding drops of blood upon the ground!

Who is this, despised, rejected,
mocked, insulted, beaten, bound?
Tis our God, Who gifts and graces
on His church is pouring down;
Who shall smite in holy vengeance
all His foes beneath His throne.

4. Who is this that hangs there dying
while the rude world scoffs and scorns,
Numbered with the malefactors,
torn with nails, and crowned with thorns?
Tis our God Who lives forever
amid the shining ones on high,
In the glorious golden city,
reigning everlastingly.

Passion Reading

The Passion of our Lord Jesus Christ according to John.

19 Then Pilate took Jesus and flogged him. 2 And the soldiers twisted together a crown of thorns and put it on his head and arrayed him in a purple robe. 3 They came up to him, saying, "Hail, King of the Jews!" and struck him with their hands. 4 Pilate went out again and said to them, "See, I am bringing him out to you that you may know that I find no guilt in him." 5 So Jesus came out, wearing the crown of thorns and the purple robe. Pilate said to them, "Behold the man!" 6 When the chief priests

and the officers saw him, they cried out, "Crucify him, crucify him!" Pilate said to them, "Take him yourselves and crucify him, for I find no guilt in him." 7 The Jews answered him, "We have a law, and according to that law he ought to die because he has made himself the Son of God." 8 When Pilate heard this statement, he was even more afraid. 9 He entered his headquarters again and said to Jesus, "Where are you from?" But Jesus gave him no answer. 10 So Pilate said to him, "You will not speak to me? Do you not know that I have authority to release you and authority to crucify you?" 11 Jesus answered him, "You would have no authority over me at all unless it had been given you from above. Therefore he who delivered me over to you has the greater sin."

12 From then on Pilate sought to release him, but the Jews cried out, "If you release this man, you are not Caesar's friend. Everyone who makes himself a king opposes Caesar." 13 So when Pilate heard these words, he brought Jesus out and sat down on the judgment seat at a place called The Stone Pavement, and in Aramaic Gabbatha. 14 Now it was the day of Preparation of the Passover. It was about the sixth hour. He said to the Jews, "Behold your King!" 15 They cried out, "Away with him, away with him, crucify him!" Pilate said to them, "Shall I crucify your King?" The chief priests answered, "We have no king but Caesar." 16 So he delivered him over to them to be crucified.

The Crucifixion

So they took Jesus, 17 and he went out, bearing his own cross, to the place called The Place of a Skull, which in Aramaic is called Golgotha. 18 There they crucified him, and with him two others, one on either side, and Jesus between them. 19 Pilate also wrote an inscription and put it on the cross. It read, "Jesus of Nazareth, the King of the Jews." 20 Many of the Jews read this inscription, for the place where Jesus was crucified was near the city, and it was written in Aramaic, in Latin, and in Greek. 21 So the chief priests of the Jews said to Pilate, "Do not write, 'The King of the Jews,' but rather, 'This man said, I am King of the Jews.'" 22 Pilate answered, "What I have written I have written."

23 When the soldiers had crucified Jesus, they took his garments and divided them into four parts, one part for each soldier; also his tunic.[d] But the tunic was seamless, woven in one piece from top to bottom, 24 so they said to one another, "Let us not tear it, but cast lots for it to see whose it shall be." This was to fulfill the Scripture which says,

> "They divided my garments among them,
>   and for my clothing they cast lots."

So the soldiers did these things, 25 but standing by the cross of Jesus were his mother and his mother's sister, Mary the wife of Clopas, and Mary Magdalene. 26 When Jesus saw his mother and the disciple whom he loved standing nearby, he said to his mother, "Woman, behold, your son!" 27 Then he said to the disciple, "Behold, your mother!" And from that hour the disciple took her to his own home.

The Death of Jesus

28 After this, Jesus, knowing that all was now finished, said (to fulfill the Scripture), "I thirst." 29 A jar full of sour wine stood there, so they put a sponge full of the sour wine on a hyssop branch and held it to his mouth. 30 When Jesus had received the sour wine, he said, "It is finished," and he bowed his head and gave up his spirit.

Jesus' Side Is Pierced

31 Since it was the day of Preparation, and so that the bodies would not remain on the cross on the Sabbath (for that Sabbath was a high day), the Jews asked Pilate that their legs might be broken and that they might be taken away. 32 So the soldiers came and broke the legs of the first, and of the other who had been crucified with him. 33 But when they came to Jesus and saw that he was already dead, they did not break his legs. 34 But one of the soldiers pierced his side with a spear, and at once there came out blood and water. 35 He who saw it has borne witness—his testimony is true, and he knows that he is telling the truth—that you also may believe. 36 For these things took place that the Scripture might be

fulfilled: "Not one of his bones will be broken." 37 And
again another Scripture says, "They will look on him
whom they have pierced."

Stricken, Smitten, and Afflicted, Thomas Kelly, 1804

Stricken, smitten, and afflicted,
See Him dying on the tree!
Tis the Christ by man rejected;
Yes, my soul, tis He, tis He!
Tis the long expected prophet,
David's Son, yet David's Lord;
Proofs I see sufficient of it:
Tis a true and faithful Word.

Tell me, ye who hear Him groaning,
Was there ever grief like His?
Friends through fear His cause disowning,
Foes insulting his distress:
Many hands were raised to wound Him,
None would interpose to save;
But the deepest stroke that pierced Him
Was the stroke that Justice gave.

Ye who think of sin but lightly,
Nor suppose the evil great
Here may view its nature rightly,
Here its guilt may estimate.
Mark the sacrifice appointed,
See who bears the awful load;

'tis the Word, the Lord's Anointed,
Son of Man and Son of God.

Here we have a firm foundation,
Here the refuge of the lost.
Christ the Rock of our salvation,
Christ the Name of which we boast.
Lamb of God for sinners wounded!
Sacrifice to cancel guilt!
None shall ever be confounded
Who on Him their hope have built.

Prayers of the People

Dear People of God: Our heavenly Father sent his Son
into the world, not to condemn the world, but that the
world through him might be saved; that all who believe in
him might be delivered from the power of sin and death,
and become heirs with him of everlasting life. We pray,
therefore, for people everywhere according to their needs.

**Almighty God, kindle, we pray, in every heart
the true love of peace, and guide with your
wisdom those who take counsel for the
nations of the earth; that in tranquility your
dominion may increase, until the earth is
filled with the knowledge of your love;
through Jesus Christ our Lord. *Amen*.**

Let us pray for all who suffer and are afflicted in body or in mind;

For the hungry and the homeless, the destitute and the oppressed
For the sick, the wounded, and the crippled
For those in loneliness, fear, and anguish
For those who face temptation, doubt, and despair
For the sorrowful and bereaved
For prisoners and captives, and those in mortal danger

That God in his mercy will comfort and relieve them, and grant them the knowledge of his love, and stir up in us the will and patience to minister to their needs.

Silence

Gracious God, the comfort of all who sorrow, the strength of all who suffer: Let the cry of those in misery and need come to you, that they may find your mercy present with them in all their afflictions; and give us, we pray, the strength to serve them for the sake of him who suffered for us, your Son Jesus Christ our Lord. *Amen*.

Let us pray for all who have not received the Gospel of Christ;

For those who have never heard the word of salvation
For those who have lost their faith
For those hardened by sin or indifference
For the contemptuous and the scornful
For those who are enemies of the cross of Christ and persecutors of his disciples
For those who in the name of Christ have persecuted others
That God will open their hearts to the truth, and lead them to faith and obedience.

Silence

Merciful God, creator of all the peoples of the earth and lover of souls: Have compassion on all who do not know you as you are revealed in your Son Jesus Christ; let your Gospel be preached with grace and power to those who have not heard it; turn the hearts of those who resist it; and bring home to your fold those who have gone astray; that there may be one flock under one shepherd, Jesus Christ our Lord.
Amen.

Let us commit ourselves to God, and pray for the grace of a holy life, that, with all who have departed this world and have died in the peace of Christ, and those whose faith is known to God alone, we may be accounted worthy to enter into the fullness of the joy of our Lord, and receive the crown of life in the day of resurrection.

Silence

O God of unchangeable power and eternal light: Look favorably on your whole Church, that wonderful and sacred mystery; by the effectual working of your providence, carry out in tranquility the plan of salvation; let the whole world
see and know that things which were cast down are being raised up, and things which had grown old are being made new, and that all things are being brought to their perfection by him through whom all things were made, your Son Jesus Christ our Lord; who lives and reigns with you, in the unity of the Holy Spirit, one God, for ever and ever. *Amen.*

O Heart Bereaved And Lonely, Fanny Crosby, late 1800s

O heart bereaved and lonely,
Whose brightest dreams have fled
Whose hopes like summer roses,
Are withered crushed and dead
Though link by link be broken,
And tears unseen may fall
Look up amid thy sorrow,
To Him who knows it all

O cling to thy Redeemer,
Thy Savior, Brother, Friend
Believe and trust His promise,

To keep you till the end
O watch and wait with patience,
And question all you will
His arms of love and mercy,
Are round about thee still

Look up, the clouds are breaking,
The storm will soon be o'er
And thou shall reach the haven,
Where sorrows are no more
Look up, be not discouraged;
Trust on, whate'er befall
Remember, O remember,
Thy Savior knows it all

Closing Prayer

Lord Jesus Christ, Son of the living God, we pray you to
set your passion, cross, and death between your judgment
and
our souls, now and in the hour of our death. Give mercy
and grace to the living; pardon and rest to the dead; to
your holy
Church peace and concord; and to us sinners everlasting
life and glory; for with the Father and the Holy Spirit you
live and reign, one God, now and for ever. Amen.

HOLY SATURDAY

LUKE 24—EASTER SUNDAY—THE RESURRECTION

JESUS SAID, "I AM THE RESURRECTION AND THE LIFE."

The Resurrection

24 BUT ON THE FIRST DAY OF THE WEEK, AT EARLY dawn, they went to the tomb, taking the spices they had prepared. 2 And they found the stone rolled away from the tomb, 3 but when they went in they did not find the body of the Lord Jesus. 4 While they were perplexed about this, behold, two men stood by them in dazzling apparel. 5 And as they were frightened and bowed their faces to the ground, the men said to them, "Why do you seek the living among the dead? 6 He is not here, but has risen. Remember how he told you, while he was still in Galilee, 7 that the Son of Man must be delivered into the hands of sinful men and be crucified and on the third day rise." 8 And they remembered his words, 9 and returning from the tomb they told all these things to the eleven and to all the rest. 10 Now it was Mary Magdalene and Joanna and Mary the mother of James and the other women with them who told these things to the apostles,

11 but these words seemed to them an idle tale, and they did not believe them. 12 But Peter rose and ran to the tomb; stooping and looking in, he saw the linen cloths by themselves; and he went home marveling at what had happened.

REFLECTIONS ON THE SEASON AND
THE SECOND COMING